MW00710984

Sobriety Handbook: The SOS Way

An Introduction to Secular Organizations for Sobriety / Save Our Selves (SOS)

First Edition, 1997

LifeRing Press

Published by LifeRing Press for the International Clearinghouse of Secular Organizations for Sobriety, 5521 Grosvenor Boulevard, Los Angeles, CA 90066. Telephone (310) 821-8430. Fax (310) 821-2610.

Secular Organizations for Sobriety, Inc., is a non-profit corporation. SECULAR ORGANIZATIONS FOR SOBRIETY is a registered trademark, and SOS and SAVE OUR SELVES are trademarks of Secular Organizations for Sobriety, Inc. Other trademarks are the property of their respective owners.

LifeRing Press and the lifering logo are trademarks of LifeRing Inc., a nonprofit corporation.

LifeRing Press
1440 Broadway, Suite 1000
Oakland, CA 94612
Tel: 510-763-0779 Fax: 510-763-1513
Email: lifering@unhooked.com
Web: www.unhooked.com/lifering/

First Edition, September 1997
ISBN 0-9659429-0-2

Cover illustration: M.C. Escher's "Drawing Hands" © 1997 Cordon Art, Baarn, Holland. All rights reserved. Used by permission.

Preface

The power to become sober is within each of us. Whether that power prevails, however, or whether we sink back into chemical enslavement may depend on the company we keep.

SOS meetings are voluntary communities of persons who feel the urgency to build new lives free of dependency on alcohol and similar drugs. SOS is one of many such efforts. Seen from afar, the SOS trend blends naturally into the broad panorama of the modern addiction recovery movement.

On closer view, SOS stands out for its lack of freight and pretense. Compared to the mainstream, these new sojourners travel light. The crowds on the old highways built more than sixty years ago stagger under a load of "Truths" so voluminous that no one could assimilate them in a lifetime. Slogans line the road like a glut of billboards, self-appointed imams hurl platitudes from all sides, contradictions and potholes buckle the pavement, there are eleven miles of detour for every mile forward, and a heavy smoke compounded of religion, spirituality, and moralism burns the eyes.

SOS has wiped the slate clean. Its founder, like a modern-day Martin Luther, but more modestly and gently, has blown away the encrustation of dogma, authoritarianism, and supernatural hocus-pocus that clogs the mainstream of contemporary "self-help." The SOS movement is a back-to-basics thing. Refresh your sobriety every day. Don't drink or use, no matter what. Make sobriety your priority in life, all the rest will follow. That's it. Or so it seems.

The first public meeting was in 1986. Since then, although still very much a minority trend, SOS has become the established alternative, the recognized No. 2, the Un-Cola.

To a casual observer, especially one coming from the traditional mindset, it may seem that there is no system or substance to the SOS approach; they may see only empty negation. Those who devote time and empathy to the organization, however, eventually discover the method beneath the madness. There is the deepest wisdom in the SOS self-empowerment approach.

SOS founder Jim Christopher's three volumes are the indispensable introduction to the SOS philosophy and spirit. The present booklet is a nuts-and-bolts guide to SOS as an organization. It grew out of a packet of guidelines that Jim C. and other early SOS members wrote for group leaders in the late 1980s in Los Angeles and distributed in photocopies. An enlarged, updated version appeared in print in 1990 as the SOS *Guidebook for Group Leaders*, now out of print.

This is a completely new text. It incorporates and updates all of the 1990 Guidebook subject matter, and goes further. Recognizing that every participant in this grassroots effort is a leader at one time or another, and that many people launch new SOS meetings without ever having attended one, the booklet is an introduction to SOS on three levels. The curious newcomer, the regular participant, and the pioneer convenor may all find useful this plain and short summary of how SOS works.

Much effort went into making the authorship of this booklet a cooperative venture. Jim C.

started the ball rolling in 1996 with the suggestion that a new edition of the 1990 Guidebook was needed. A first draft was posted for SOS convenors on the Internet in the second half of 1996, and comments were collected by email. Participants in the SOS *UU in the Pines IV* retreat in March 1997 reviewed and discussed a second draft at a workshop. Two further drafts were posted on the Internet for convenors and members of the SOS email list.

Many hands have worked here. The drafts of Chapters 1-5 are by Marty N.; Chapter 6 is by Tom Shelley with additional material by Laura L. A section of Chapter 1 is quoted from an SOS International Newsletter article by Janis B. The draft letter to professionals is by Nick J. Comments, suggestions, and contributions to the content have been received from Jim C., Ed B., Dick S., Jim M., Tim B., Mark P., Jan B., Sarah P., Bill L., Paula B., Mike F., Karl S., Dudley A., Craig M., Nick J., Don B., Ron C., John D., Bill C., Jane T., Maxine C., Lisa E., Linda C., Larry B., Aram A., Kerrie M., Rick G., Mark P., Larry D., Michael O., Sherry F., Ben B., and others. Cindy in Maine, Mog in New York, Leigh in Oakland, Ben in Georgia and Mark in Florida nailed typos and stylistic inconsistencies in the final draft, via the Internet. Lisa E. of Oakland consulted on typography and cover design. We are particularly grateful to Jim C., the founder of SOS, for his thorough review of the manuscript and his many valuable suggestions.

In keeping with the self-help theme so fundamental to SOS -- it stands at its core for "Save Our Selves" -- this booklet has been self-published. LifeRing Press was formed specifically to mobilize the endogenous talents and resources of SOS for this project. Excepting the printer, everyone who has worked on this book is in recovery from a substance addiction, and all have donated their labor.

With current technology, updating a text is easier than ever. Whether you are squeaky new to sobriety, or are an old salt who has been sober longer than the drinking age, or somewhere in-between, we hope to hear your comments, suggestions and contributions for inclusion in future editions of this handbook. May this booklet be a companion of your sober life for many years.

-- *The Publisher*

Table of Contents

Underneath the diversity of SOS meetings, they all have three things in common: they are secular, they are abstinent, and they are self-help.

The story of Bob, Elizabeth, Norma, Janie, Mort, and other fictionalized members and visitors as they explore what secularity, abstinence, and self-help mean in the real life of the meetings.

The only reliable sobriety program for you is one that you construct yourself. Why we reject prefabricated capital-P Programs and embrace self-empowerment sobriety. Our meetings as program-building workshops.

You may want some tools for building your sobriety program. Here is a sampler of sobriety tools from the founder and from convenors and meeting participants.

What happens at a meeting? Advantages of sharing and crosstalk. The topic system. Leadership positions and rotation. How to handle money.

Chapter Six: How To Start an SOS Meeting, 71

Nuts and bolts of finding a meeting space, welcoming new members, and getting the word out about SOS sobriety meetings.

Appendix, 81

Introduction

Alcoholism and other substance addictions kill hundreds of thousands of people in the United States each year, and rob millions of the full enjoyment of their lives. It has been estimated that as many as one out of ten Americans has a serious problem with alcohol and/or other addictive substances.

Only a small fraction of the people whose lives are seriously harmed by alcohol are helped by the efforts of the oldest and largest self-help organization, Alcoholics Anonymous (AA) and its 12-Step offshoots. For reasons that are now history, the founders of AA gave their movement a pronounced religious orientation, which is readily apparent today to visitors at a typical AA meeting. The organization's religious cast turns many people away at the door. Many who do enter remain deeply uncomfortable with the group's compulsory religiosity and yearn for a freer, broader environment.

SOS was formed in 1986 in response to the widely felt need for an organization that could provide the benefits of the self-help process without the burdens of the 12-Step dogma. We are now more than ten years old. What began as a brave and scary experiment is now a tried and established method. We are still small, but we have a track record of success, we enjoy national and international recognition, and we have a growing number of SOS "sobrietists" whose sober lives are testimonials to what we do.

Although begun by alcoholics, SOS welcomes all persons seeking to end a chemical dependency or compulsion, including overeaters, persons with dual diagnosis, and many others, as well as their families and friends. SOS has come to stand for Secular Support generally.

Addiction strikes men and women of every nationality, culture, race, sexual orientation, language, class, and ethnic background. SOS welcomes all who wish to get and stay sober, and treasures diversity. SOS has no room for sexual harassment, nor for religious, racial, national, or other invidious intolerance.

The structure of SOS meetings is flexible, and there is ample room for a variety of meetings, such as those focused on families and friends (codependents), gay and lesbian issues, African-American issues, Latino issues, lifestyle issues, and any other issues that can bond a group in sobriety.

This introductory handbook necessarily emphasizes the fundamentals. Real life often presents advanced problems that require creativity and flexibility in applying the basics. You, the group members, are free to experiment, to modify and innovate, to shape your SOS meeting to fit your needs. If you have a different way to build on the common foundations of SOS, something that works for you in your situation, by all means share it with others; perhaps your approach will find its way into the next edition of this handbook.

CHAPTER ONE
COMMON FOUNDATIONS

The members of each SOS meeting are free to work out its structure and format. Each group is autonomous in its everyday functioning. Groups even in the same locality may have distinctly different flavors and atmospheres. Meetings may vary from week to week. But underneath all this flux and diversity, all SOS meetings have a common foundation: they are secular, they are sober, and they are self-help. These are our three S's. It is important that all group members understand and reach consensus on these basic principles, and become skillful in applying them and protecting them in a variety of situations.

[1] *Secular*

The first word in our name is "Secular." Webster's defines "secular" as "pertaining to the world or to things not spiritual or sacred; relating to or connected with worldly things; disassociated from religious teachings or principles; not devoted to sacred or religious use; temporal; nonecclesiastical; worldly; as, *secular* education, *secular* music." Applied to our meetings, secular means that we separate sobriety from religion. We do not ask our members to adhere to any religious beliefs as part of their recovery process. We do not practice prayer or other religious observances at our meetings. We do not ask members to recognize or to select or to surrender to any "Higher Power." We do not require or suggest that they undergo a religious or spiritual "awakening" or conversion experience. We do not ask them to seek, or to rely on, supernatural help in getting sober or in improving their character. We do not suggest to our members that the credit for their sobriety belongs to anyone but themselves. That is the meaning of "secular."

"Secular" is not the same as "atheist" or "agnostic." Although SOS has many members who do not practice any organized religion, and many who consider themselves atheists or agnostics, there are also members who attend church regularly and who have clearly defined, firm religious beliefs. They prefer SOS because SOS does not require them to amend or compromise their religion, or to acquire a second religion on top of their first. Neither religion nor anti-religion are usual topics of conversation at an SOS meeting.

SOS is not similar to an "atheist-agnostic" meeting within AA. For AA, atheists and agnostics are imperfect creatures who must first be brought to believe in a God before they can become sober. SOS, by contrast, cherishes people as they are, regardless of their religious belief or disbelief, and teaches that all those who wish to become clean and sober can do so.

Belonging to SOS, in summary, is somewhat like belonging to a sports team. Most sports teams are secular. It does not matter what religion you are, or whether you are any at all. Nobody thinks to ask. Everybody is free to be what they want to be. Nobody is so rude as to try to convert or preach. All that anybody cares about is, can you play. Likewise in SOS. Your religious beliefs are not an issue; nobody will ask, nobody will preach. All that anybody cares is, are you sober.

[2] *Sober*

In SOS, sobriety means complete abstinence from alcohol and other mind-altering addictive drugs. Sobriety means staying clear of the substance to which we are addicted, as well as staying clear of other mind-altering addictive drugs. If we're alcoholics, we stay away from booze as well as other mind-altering addictive drugs. If we're dope addicts, we stay away from narcotics and controlled substances as well as alcohol. We choose "across the board" sobriety.

To some who come to SOS meetings intrigued by the world "alternative" or "option," this hard-line definition of sobriety is disturbing. Perhaps some hope that SOS will have found a way to make "social drinking" or "controlled drinking" or "moderation" possible, when in fact all responsible recovery programs share this requirement of total abstinence. For SOS, sobriety defined as total abstinence is the logical, rational foundation of recovery.

Currently on the market are a few books by "scientists" seeking to revolutionize recovery by "proving" that the process of addiction can be reversed, or cured, or that it doesn't exist to begin with. There are always a few who believe that the experiences of hundreds of thousands of alcoholics have been misdiagnosed, mistreated, misnamed.

SOS views alcoholism and addiction in a realistic, rational light. Most of us know first hand that "cutting down" or "drinking moderately" simply doesn't work for us. We may not fully understand the physiological workings of our condition, but we do know that if we don't drink or use, we stay sober.

Sober, we can use our minds for clear, logical thinking and problem-solving. Sober, we can reach out in confidence to others in SOS for help when we need it. Sober, we can offer real help to someone who needs us. Sober, at least we have a chance.

SOS is about secular sobriety. While each meeting's format and special interests are of their own choosing, it is incumbent upon group leaders to ensure that those who attend, particularly newcomers, are aware of what SOS means by "sobriety." It's a basic concept, simple to convey and of vital importance to the consistency and continuity of SOS as a whole.

[3] *Self-Help*

All SOS groups are self-help groups. That is, there is no physician, therapist, counselor, or other professional in charge, or lurking at the door passing out business cards. Leadership is by peers: group leaders are ordinary alcoholics and addicts, the same as the group members. No special training is required. If physicians or other professionals do attend, it is either by special invitation as observers, or because they are themselves addicts and alcoholics, and in that case they are there in their capacity as recovering addicts and not as providers of treatment.

On occasion, lay persons who are not alcoholics or addicts have helped SOS meetings get started, and many people who are not personally affected by alcohol or drugs are friends and supporters of our movement. But persons who deny any significant problem with alcohol or drugs in their own lives or in their relationships would not have a long-term role in an SOS meeting. Our meetings are fundamentally mutual assistance communities: we are alcoholics and addicts Saving Our Selves.

Self-help also means that group leaders and members normally refrain from offering amateur medical advice or psychotherapy to each other. We don't tell people what to do. We don't give advice unless a person expressly asks for it. Instead, the members share their own experiences and understandings, their personal failures and victories. In time, the new member begins to discover what is needed to fit their particular situation.

Self-help is also a question of economics. No SOS group charges a fee or requires a contribution. Most do pass a basket for voluntary contributions to defray the organization's expenses, and each meeting is financially self-supporting.

Self-help also means that the meetings avoid outside entanglements. SOS meetings may rent space from hospitals, churches, libraries, banks, and other entities, but they are autonomous from and avoid affiliation with any such institutions. SOS meetings are not affiliated with any political party or movement. Their only affiliation is with each other and with the national and international SOS organizations.

Self-help connects with and reinforces our first principle, secularity. We rely on ourselves and on each other, not on some external "Higher Power," for assistance in our work of getting and staying sober.

The power of self-help meetings is widely recognized. For the person newly struggling with an alcohol or drug problem, the self-help meeting may be the one anchor in their currently stormy existence. In the meeting, the person can acknowledge their problem openly without fear of harm or

ridicule. In the meeting, we get encouragement
for our fledgling efforts at sobriety in the midst of
an uncaring world. We get complete understanding and acceptance, warts and all. We may con-
fide for the first time the things in our life of
which we feel guilty or ashamed, or which en-
raged us, and in so doing, we discharge the
poison in those feelings. By listening to others, we
learn to forgive ourselves. By speaking, we gain
clues to what we think. By sharing our feelings,
we change them, and so we gradually change
ourselves. We pick up tools and techniques, new
information, new ideas. We may learn social skills
that withered when the bottle was our only
"friend." We may catch up with stages of our
emotional development that were arrested during
our addiction. We may repair a shattered self
image and rebuild a devastated self-esteem. We
may let the air out of an ego that is over-inflated.
We may come to like ourselves again. In time, we
may develop empathy, compassion, new friendships, new interests, new loves, new careers, new
lives. We've all seen it happen.

CHAPTER TWO
CASE STUDIES IN THE
COMMON FOUNDATIONS

Case studies illustrate a point better than generalizations. Here are some case studies inspired by events in actual SOS meetings. The names have been changed and in some cases the facts have been combined or rearranged, the better to illustrate the point. By analyzing these cases, we will be able to grasp the principle involved more concretely, and will be able to apply it to the new and different situations that constantly arise in life. Maybe your group has thought of a different and better way to handle these situations. If so, please send it in so that others can benefit from your experience.

[A] Cases in Secularity

(1) Bob, a newcomer to the SOS meeting, shared that he has been having great difficulty staying sober and that he was planning to do the Twelve Steps. He paused and looked around the room, then said he believed in God.

Newcomers sometimes confuse SOS meetings with AA meetings. Unsure of their surroundings, they repeat the things they have heard in AA meetings and that earn them approval there. How should a group respond to this sort of statement? The group leader in this instance said that if Bob felt that doing the Steps was the way for him personally to stay sober, then more power to him.

Other group members nodded agreement. The group leader then picked up on the secular kernel of Bob's concern, namely his frequent relapses, and shared a relapse experience she had had. Other group members contributed their own relapse or near-relapse stories and told of techniques they used to recognize and deal with their personal pre-relapse warning flags. The topic of discussion thus moved smoothly off religion and onto sobriety. The group leader handled the issue well. Bob did not feel attacked for his statements and he got useful knowledge for staying sober, if he wanted it. Whether Bob stays in SOS or goes off to AA or continues go to both meetings is not so important. What matters is that Bob got support and ammunition for his desire to stay sober.

(2) Elizabeth, a woman in her 50s attending her third SOS meeting, volunteered to act as chair and to introduce a topic for the evening's discussion. She said her topic was the Serenity Prayer, because she was constantly stressed out by her adult son's active cocaine addiction.

The group leader led off the sharing, telling of an experience he had had with his own teenage son and the concern he felt that the son might become an alcoholic like his father. Other group members picked up the parent-child theme and added their shares. Elizabeth's real concern was not the Serenity Prayer but her son and the guilt she felt at perhaps being responsible for his addiction, and the group leader deftly reframed the discussion around that secular topic. Elizabeth was not made to feel uncomfortable for her religious statements. The group's sharing struck a chord with Elizabeth and she came away from the meeting feeling supported and relieved of some of her stress. At the end, the group leader recognized Elizabeth's initiative for having chaired a meeting, and called on other group members to step forward likewise and sign up to chair future meetings.

(3) A first-time visitor to the meeting listened in silence for twenty minutes and then launched into a monologue, which began like this: "I got sober through our Lord and Savior Jesus Christ and I've been listening so far and I haven't heard one person say they did too. There is a funky vibe in this meeting, with people seeming to think they can get sober without God; that's impossible. It says in Step Two ..." and so on.

The group leader let it go on for half a minute, at which point the visitor started repeating himself and getting heated up. At that point she cut him off, and said, "Excuse me, but it's obvious that you've accidentally landed in the wrong meeting. This is an SOS sobriety meeting where we don't do religious preaching. You wanted an AA meeting; it meets in this room on a different night. Now if you'll excuse us, we'd like to continue our sobriety meeting." This visitor was rude; he crossed the line between sharing a personal religious experience, which is OK, and advocating a religious path to sobriety, which is misplaced. The individual had no sobriety experience to share; his main concern was to promote his religious program. The group leader correctly intervened to protect the secular character of the meeting. As the visitor left, muttering, group members observed how the visitor had elevated religion higher than sobriety and failed to show respect for sobriety no matter how it was achieved.

(4) Lenny had spent several months in AA meetings and was very angry. At his first SOS meeting, he confided that he hated the Sunday School atmosphere of AA and "all that bullshit religious crap." He went on venting his feelings for some time, and invited the meeting to take up the topic of criticizing AA's religious approach, beginning with the eight mentions of "God" in the Twelve Steps.

The group leader, knowing that Lenny was new, let him vent his frustration and share his experiences for a while. But she intervened when Lenny attempted to sidetrack the whole meeting into a put-down of the AA approach. "We're here to work on our own sobriety, not to shoot down how other people work on theirs," she said. She then turned the discussion to the topic of dealing with frustration and anger, always a lively theme. Lenny felt better; he had a chance to vent, and there had been things shared in the ensuing "anger" discussion that he found thought-provoking. The group leader protected the secular character of the meeting by turning discussion away from an anti-religion theme toward a secular sobriety topic.

[B] Cases in Sobriety

(1) Charles introduced himself at his first SOS meeting as an "AA reject" who got "sick and tired" of AA's harping on the theme of lifelong abstinence. He had heard that SOS was an alternative to AA and he was here to get support for his efforts to learn to drink in moderation. He felt that just having two drinks a day was a more realistic goal for him than trying to be abstinent.

The group members looked knowingly at one another, and finally one member began: "I used to want to learn to drink in moderation, too. I would start every evening with that idea in mind, and every night after the first drink I would forget about it and get drunk." Every other group member shared similar stories. "If I could learn to drink in moderation, I wouldn't be an alcoholic and I wouldn't be here," was the consensus. There was much humorous discussion about what constituted "two drinks." Finally the group leader gently but firmly suggested that if Charles was stuck on the idea of trying moderation, he should find a different organization than SOS. As far as the need for lifelong abstinence went, the views of AA and SOS were exactly the same, she pointed out. Charles did not come back. Possibly the fact that two such divergent organizations as SOS and AA had the same view on this basic issue made an impression on him that he may remember later, if he can remember anything at all, after his moderation experiments fail.

(2) Norma had gone to SOS meetings for quite a while without saying much. This evening there had been sharing about marijuana use, and Norma offered that she had smoked the weed off and on for years, and never had any problem stopping and never had withdrawal symptoms. Since marijuana was not addictive for her, she didn't see any reason why she shouldn't use it now and then when she felt like it.

The group almost jumped on Norma. Almost everyone in the group had used marijuana at one time or another, and felt strongly that smoking marijuana was the same kind of "drug escape cop-out" as drinking alcohol. Most people reported that they had usually smoked and drunk at the same time; that one had been a powerful trigger for the other; and that smoking weed was incompatible with thinking soberly. The idea that one could call themselves "sober" while using marijuana struck group members like fingernails on a chalkboard. Before the atmosphere got too hostile toward Norma, the group leader intervened and read aloud from the "Principles of SOS," which says "Sobriety is the number one priority in an alcoholic's or addict's life. *As such, they must abstain from all drugs or alcohol.*" He then asked Norma if she wanted to say anything. Norma said she would think about it. Discussion turned to other topics. A few meetings later, Norma said she had decided that marijuana didn't really mean anything to her anyway, that it was a stupid risk to run, and that she was going to forget about it and stay clean and sober "all the way." She got applause and hugs all around.

(3) Mort had been quiet for a long time. He had confided in one of his friends that he had had a drink. At the meeting, this friend now asked Mort if he didn't want to share something that had happened in his sobriety. Mort then said he didn't but if the group insisted, he would. He said that he used to think of himself as an alcoholic, but he had been sober for four years now and if he had really ever been an alcoholic, he was no longer one; he was "cured." He said he had had a glass of wine for dinner last month, and felt no ill effects, and was planning to do it again whenever he felt like it. He felt that abstinence was necessary for people in early sobriety, but once you were "advanced" like he was, you could control your drinking like normal people.

Mort was an old-time member who had made many contributions in the past. To hear that Mort had relapsed came as a heavy blow. Everyone was too stunned to speak. Finally the group leader broke the silence to share that the struggle against denial inside of her was an ongoing issue, and that she expected it would remain a live issue until she died. "Alcoholism is a cunning, tireless foe who can easily lie in wait for a decade or more, waiting for the opportunity to reclaim its victim. As we accumulate sober time, we can get complacent and forget about our addiction, and then we relapse into drinking and into denial of our alcoholism." She urged Mort to call her or any other member whenever he felt an urge to drink, or to get professional help if that was not enough for him. The group expressed to Mort how much they valued him and how much his sobriety meant to each of them. Mort said sarcastically he appreciated their concern but that he was cured now and his drinking was none of their business. He stopped coming to meetings. A few months later he showed up at a public gathering unsteady, with the front of his pants wet, smelling of beer and urine; a security guard had to escort him out. Two and a half years later he was in the obituaries. He had put himself beyond the power of the group, or of anyone, to help him.

(4) Cathy had been clean and sober for sixteen months, and the group had elected her secretary of the meeting. Now it was time for Cathy to go on vacation. She chose to return to a vacation spot in Mexico where she used to go and get drunk when she was drinking. The group shared with her that going back to heavy wet spots was risky behavior, but she went anyway. When she returned, she admitted to the group that on the last night, she had "slipped" and had three Margaritas. She now felt awful about it and swore she would never go back

to that spot again and would be more careful in her behavior in the future. She felt she had learned an important lesson. She also felt that since she had only a few days' sober time now, she should not serve as group leader at this time, and asked the group to elect someone else.

Group members welcomed Cathy back and made a point of saying that they were very glad that she had shared her experience with the group immediately and openly. Several people shared their own relapse experiences, saying that they had become wiser and stronger in their sobriety because of it. There was a consensus that group leaders should have a significant amount of sober time, and so Cathy's resignation was accepted and Sally was voted secretary in her place. Cathy remained a loved, valued, and sober member of the meeting and was re-elected as group secretary six months later. She has been sober ever since.

(5) Harry came to the SOS meeting with alcohol on his breath. As part of the opening statement, the group secretary read the sentence "If you are under the influence of alcohol now, we ask that you maintain silence at this meeting." Harry blurted out, "Well, I better shaddup then." But "shaddup" he could not. At his third interruption, the group leader asked him to leave, and he did.

It's impossible to gain any benefit from the group self-help process while under the influence of alcohol or drugs. If a person insists on attending anyway, they must keep silent -- no speaking, moaning, singing, snickering, or other participation. If they can't follow this rule, out they go on the spot. If they won't leave on their own steam, members need to either call a security person, if one is available, or cancel the meeting. Members should not use physical force to eject the person; to do so could incur legal liability in case of injury. It would be a big mistake to tolerate meeting participation by persons who are anything but completely clean and sober at that time. Harry is welcome to come back when he is sober, but he must be made to understand that he will be out in the cold while he is under the influence. To allow him to participate would discredit the group and destroy its process, without helping Harry in the slightest. The group leader handled the situation correctly.

(6) Jim and Diane came to SOS meetings newly sober and participated actively for a year and a half. Jim and Diane recognized early, clearly, and openly that they were both alcoholics and that abstinence was the only way out for them. They worked on the problems in their relationship in the meetings and also outside with professional counselors. They came to a better understanding of each other, and got a lot of satisfaction from the improvement in their lives. They found new success in their careers and new satisfaction in their roles as parents. Eventually they said a friendly good bye to their meetings and stopped coming. Members run into them occasionally at the auto parts store that Jim manages, and always have a friendly chat; Jim even gives his SOS friends a "mechanic's discount." Recently they marked their third anniversary of sobriety. They dropped in at the SOS Sober New Year's Eve party and shared old times with their friends who still attend regularly.

Jim and Diane found a new support system to take the place of their SOS meetings -- each other. Although many couples break up during the recovery of one of them, these two regularly came to meetings together and also got professional help, and came out stronger. They continue to acknowledge their alcoholism and continue good relations with their SOS friends. Sobriety has brought them important real-life payoffs in their careers and as parents, and this doesn't hurt. Their meetings remember them fondly, and the door is always open should one or both want to come back.

[C] Cases in Self-Help

(1) Janie was a newcomer and sat silently twisting a strand of her hair through most of the sharing time. The topic was friendships. When she finally got up the courage to speak, she shared that she wanted hard to be sober, but the old friend that she always hung out with after work was a heavy drinker and pressured her to drink too, for friendship's sake. "I feel like such a pill if I don't drink with her," Janie sighed, "and she's been my best friend for years." "Oh, that's easy," blurted out Roberta, another group member, "I know what you need to do! Just tell her to get lost and you go find another friend."

Ouch! Double ouch! It was the rule in this meeting -- laid out in the opening statement -- that during sharing time, nobody responds directly to another person's statements. Roberta's remark was a direct response to Janie's share, and violated the meeting's process. If Roberta wanted to engage Janie in dialogue, she needed to wait until the time set aside for crosstalk, usually the last ten to fifteen minutes of the meeting.

Roberta's remark also violated a more basic rule of the self-help process by offering unsolicited advice. Janie hadn't asked for advice, she merely shared her feelings. Janie now felt judged; she felt that Roberta was attacking her for being loyal to her friend. Janie was saying to herself, "Oh yeah? Who appointed *you* my mother? If I want advice, I'll pay for it. You think it's so easy to dump a friend? I can tell what kind of friend *you* are. I'll tell you who's going to get lost and find another friend, and that's me from this meeting." It's unfortunate that Janie was too timid to speak her thoughts out loud; the whole meeting could have learned from them. Here, all the group leader could do to salvage the situation was to quickly remind Roberta "let's save it for crosstalk" and move on to the next share, so that Janie could try to settle her feelings. If Roberta is the group leader, the meeting is in trouble.

Let's try it again.

(2) *Janie was a newcomer and sat silently twisting a strand of her hair through most of the sharing time. The topic was friendships. When she finally got up the courage to speak, she shared that she wanted hard to be sober, but the old friend that she always hung out with after work was a heavy drinker and pressured her to drink too, for friendship's sake. "I feel like such a pill if I don't drink with her," Janie sighed, "and she's been my best friend for years." Roberta, who hadn't shared yet, then said "Oh, that resonates with an experience I had." Roberta then told the story of a boyfriend she had when she was trying to get sober, who used all kinds of pressure tactics on her to get drunk with him. She put up with it for months, but one day in bed she told him that she was perfectly happy to*

*see him, but only if he came to her sober. He
answered that he didn't like her sober. Then she
threw him out. Everybody laughed.*

Roberta got it right this time. She didn't pre-
sume to know the answer to Janie's problem. She
didn't set herself up as parent, priest, psychia-
trist, judge, or some other kind of authority over
Janie. She didn't try to control Janie's life. She
empathized with Janie's dilemma and respected
Janie's intelligence in handling it. She allowed
Janie to construct a solution to Janie's problem
by herself. She didn't address Janie directly at
all, other than to say that Janie's story resonated
with something she had experienced. She didn't
use controlling terms like "you should" or "you
have to." She used sharing terms like "I did" or
"this happened to me." Janie, in turn, felt good
after having shared her feelings. She felt that her
own sharing was valuable because it stimulated
another member, Roberta, to share something
similar. She felt that she was among people who
had similar experiences and who understood and
accepted her, and this made her feel safe. She
delighted in Roberta's sharing of intimate details,
and felt encouraged to do the same next time.
She felt Roberta was smart and fair and would
make a good friend. Roberta's story gave Janie
the idea that she might ask her own friend to go
out sober once, to see what would happen.
Guessing the answer in advance, Janie began on
her own to form the plan to stop seeing that
friend. A few months later, Janie did break up
with that friend. She then shared: "She wasn't
really my friend. Her only real friend was the
bottle. Now I go to a gym instead and work out,
and I feel much better. And I've got new friends
who are sober."

(3) Myrna was a busy, efficient person who was good at organizational details. She volunteered to help organize an SOS picnic, and was diligent at making phone calls and setting up all the necessary arrangements. Fairly soon other members were relying on her to take care of the business details of the two meetings she attended, and she did a very good job. Before long she knew everyone and everything, and took good care of whatever needed doing in her quiet, helpful manner, so that people remarked they did not know how they ever got along before Myrna came. She said little at meetings, but she gradually disclosed that she was lonely, that her two Chihuahuas were her closest companions, that she valued the good fellowship of the meetings, and that doing organizational chores made her feel socially relevant. It was quite some time before the other members of the meeting realized that Myrna had never had an alcohol or substance abuse problem of any kind, and was not involved in a relationship with anyone who did. She was simply lonely and loved being helpful to others.

Although we value sociability and good fellowship, we are not a social club. SOS is a self-help organization for people who are trying to overcome their own problems with alcohol or drugs, or who are involved in relationships where alcohol or drugs are a problem. The main purpose of our meetings is for us to work on our addiction problems and to give each other support in that specific effort. We share freely at our meetings because we know that those who hear us are people like ourselves. Our sharing resonates because the room is filled with empathetic souls. The support we get has special value for us because it comes from others who have been there and done that. We do not come to self-help meetings to solicit the sympathy of the general public for our condition.

Thus, while we may welcome the unafflicted as an occasional guest, we cannot do our work unfettered except in the exclusive company of others like ourselves.

An important part of our recovery work is to tend to our own organizational survival. Performing service tasks for the meetings teaches us to retake responsibility for our lives and gives us an opportunity to practice sobriety-oriented behavior. Service tasks also often involve elements of leadership and control, and these are not matters we can leave to others if we wish to Save Our Selves. All of our leadership is by our peers. A group led by persons who deny any personal problem with substance addiction, no matter how kindly their intention, would not be a member group of SOS. For these reasons, the meeting secretary, after informally discussing the matter privately with other regulars at the meeting, took Myrna aside one evening and very gently and lovingly explained to her that she needed to find another kind of group to be helpful to. It was difficult for Myrna at first, but she got the point and in a warm and tearful moment said her good-byes to the meeting. She was missed, and some service tasks were neglected for a while until the members stepped in and picked up the slack themselves and put things right. A few months later a member happened to meet Myrna on the street. She was radiant; she had become a volunteer at the local SPCA. She had found a new and presumably more grateful set of beneficiaries of her charity.

CHAPTER THREE
THE SOS PROGRAM

In ancient Greek mythology there was a roadside bandit named Procrustes who had a bed in which he forced all travelers to lie. Those who were shorter than the bed, he stretched until their bones cracked; those who were longer, he cut off their feet.

Most alcoholism and addiction programs are like Procrustes and his bed. Everyone has "The Program": one size fits all. In AA, everyone does the Twelve Steps. In Rational Recovery, everyone does AVRT. In SMART, everyone does REBT. And so on. Each vendor promises that its particular Program is the Answer. In fact, some people are helped by the Steps, some are not, and the same is true of the others. There is no such thing as one Program that works for everybody, and we doubt there will ever be.

SOS is unique in the alcoholism and addiction movement in deliberately *not* offering a capital-P Program. We have no Program, no panacea, no one-size-fits-all, no cookie cutter, no miracle cure, no magic pill to sell. We reject the whole dichotomy between Program and alcoholic, in which The Program is the active, knowing, healthy protagonist and the alcoholic or addict is the passive, dumb, sick raw material to be stamped and molded into the desired shape. We think that any approach that acts on the alcoholic over time as an outside compulsion, a Program, is doomed to fail with most of the people most of the time.

No program, including the SOS self-empowerment approach, will work if the person doesn't have an inner desire to escape from addiction. SOS rests its entire chance of success on the encouragement and rational nurture of that desire.

We hold that each alcoholic or addict needs to construct their own sobriety based on their own experiences and needs. We think each alcoholic not only needs to, but is able to construct his or her own personal sobriety program, if afforded the support and the tools. The work of putting a program together must be and is done by the newly recovering persons themselves, just as each of us with long-term sobriety has done it for ourselves. We have confidence in the ability of alcoholics and addicts, no matter how serious our history, to pull ourselves together with peer group support. We have seen it work. Conversely, we are quite certain that we cannot get and stay sober unless we construct a sobriety program for ourselves. That is why we say that we have no one (big-P) Program; we have as many programs (small p) as we have participants.

Our main "program construction workshop" consists of the friendly environment of our secular self-help meetings. The protective, non-judgmental atmosphere, the ability to express oneself honestly and frankly, the companionship of other sober alcoholics with their funds of experience and wit, form our principal nourishment and our toolbox. In this environment, the newly sober person soon gains the self-confidence and the commonsense skills to avoid the most glaring relapse traps. In time, we learn that we can unload our painful emotions by sharing them, that we can handle agonizing memories by sharing them, that we can resist the seduction of our addiction by disclosing it at meetings. We learn that we can recover from

relapse if we get back "in" immediately and acknowledge it openly. We learn little slogans to help
organize our thoughts, such as "we don't drink or
use, no matter what," or "Sobriety Priority" and
others. We read books and articles and get new
ideas about our condition. We read about the
personal programs of others, and borrow something, or not. We may practice little helpful tricks,
such as daily affirmation exercises, or medita-
tions, or changes in our diet, recreation, or other
behavior. We may scavenge a bit of wisdom from
other programs, and add it to our construct. And
then, one day at a meeting, the topic is "How I
Stay Sober." We share with the meeting what
exactly we do. We weren't really aware of it until
then, but we have constructed our own sobriety
program. It is us and we are it. No one else has a
program precisely like this one. It works for me
because I built it myself; I know it intimately; I
own it and I operate it; I made it; it is mine.

The big-P Programs are by their nature dis-
empowering. If the alcoholic mentally surrenders
to them, adopts them, and manages somehow to
stay sober through them, all the credit goes to The
Program. The recovering person brought nothing
to the table; their effort was worth zero. The
Program got them sober; The Program is Great. If
things happen that The Program didn't foresee,
they are in deep trouble. They remain dependent
on The Program, and become personally threat-
ened and incensed if The Program is criticized.

The SOS approach is just the opposite. If the
alcoholic or addict, having constructed their own
program, remains clean and sober, all of the credit
goes to the individual and boosts their self-esteem
and confidence. The recovering person's own effort
was everything. Having constructed their program
themselves, they have the skill to modify or extend
it to meet unexpected situations. They are inde-

pendent and self-sustaining. If SOS is criticized, they don't get defensive. If someone blasts SOS for not having The Program, they cheerfully agree, baffling the attacker. They may love SOS and feel grateful to it, they may continue to attend meetings for many years, they may give their time and money to make it available to others, but they aren't dependent on it or powerless without it.

When you are an SOS group leader, your responsibilities are different than as a group leader in other programs. There, you need to surrender to The Program so that you can master it and impose it on others. You need to memorize The Program's encrusted dogma so that you can recite its catch-phrases at the appropriate moments. If you are good at that, you may be rewarded with a title such as "Sponsor" or "Facilitator" or "Technician," and you can lord it over the unwashed, and maybe make money.

Here in SOS your job is not to impose a Program on the members but to protect the foundations of SOS so that the members have a safe space for their own program-building activity. You are the guardian of the meeting's process; and part of that job is to protect the group against any effort to impose The Program on it or to erect an encrusted dogma to memorize. You will never get a title or power or money from your leadership. Your only reward will be that for those few months when it was your turn to lead, the other participants in your meeting made good progress in constructing their sobriety programs, and so did you. If, at the end of your term, they are not even aware that anyone was in charge, and believe that everything happened completely by itself and by their own doing, you did your job well.

CHAPTER FOUR:
A SOBRIETY RESOURCE KIT

Each of us has to construct our own sobriety program. As we start this work, one of the first things we may do is to look at the ways that other people have built theirs. We call the various ideas, devices, tricks, tips, methods, insights, and other ways that people use to stay sober "sobriety tools." This chapter collects some of the tools that other SOS members have found or made, and have used for themselves with good success.

As you read these ideas, keep three things in mind.

One: none of these is compulsory for you. There are SOS members who stay sober without using any particular device that they can identify; they just don't drink, period. Whatever works to keep you sober is right for you.

Two: this collection is not exhaustive. There are many other tools, and people invent new ones all the time. So, listen up, look around, read, experiment, and you'll likely hit on other good ideas not mentioned here. If you do, won't you send them in, for the next edition of this handbook?

The third thing to keep in mind is that no tool is any good unless you use it. The tools are not just for contemplating; they require some change in behavior. As we change our behavior, we gain new insights, and these insights help us make further changes in behavior. Staying clean and sober may be the greatest behavior change in our lives.

1. Jim Christopher's 'Cycle of Addiction' and 'Cycle of Sobriety'

Jim Christopher, the founder of SOS, has published three books that contain a wealth of different sobriety tools. They are *How To Stay Sober -- Recovery Without Religion* (1988); *Unhooked: Staying Sober and Drug-Free* (1989); and *SOS Sobriety – The Proven Alternative to 12-Step Programs* (1992). These works contain tools that Jim C. developed and found effective in his own personal recovery (he has been sober since April 24, 1978), as well as tools that he collected from others and passed along. You should read those books to get the full concept. Information on where to obtain them is in the Appendix. In this brief Handbook, you can only get the gist of the idea.

For Jim, getting sober means replacing the "Cycle of Addiction" with the "Cycle of Sobriety." The Cycle of Addiction consists of three debilitating elements. One: chemical need – craving for the drug at the cellular level, physiological addiction, whether genetically inherited or acquired. Two: learned habit – our set of chronic drinking or using patterns and associations. Three: denial of need and habit – our mental gymnastics by which we hide from ourselves (if from no one else) that we have become addicted. As we go deeper into the addiction, it gradually becomes "Priority One" in our everyday lives. We work, eat, socialize, think, and fantasize for one purpose only, and that is to feed our addiction.

The "Cycle of Sobriety" is a personal recovery program that elevates sobriety to the role of top priority in our lives. In lieu of the daily cycle of cellular craving, habit, and denial, Jim places a three-part cycle of getting real. This consists of daily acknowledgement of one's addiction to alcohol or drugs, daily acceptance of one's addiction, and daily prioritization of sobriety as the primary issue in one's life, *separate from anything else.*

Jim C. labels his approach "cognitive-visceral synchronization," meaning that it aims to bring our visceral feelings into harmony with our rational understanding. Our "gut" tends to drive us into relapse, especially in the early period, even though we understand in our minds that drinking will harm us. In order to heal and reclaim our injured survival system, Jim emphasizes the need for daily, emotionally impactful reaffirmation of our sobriety priority.

Many of the sobriety tools SOS members use are varieties of this "Daily Do." See Part 3 of this chapter. The daily reaffirmations of our sobriety over time break up the old addictive associations and create new patterns that fortify our sobriety.

Jim's C.'s *Triumph!* Relapse Prevention Workshops (available separately) are an intensive application of the daily cognitive-visceral synchronization concept. The aim of these exercises is to retrain our primitive survival system. Jim theorizes that our addictive cravings stem at the deepest level from a primitive segment of our brain, the limbic system, which humans have in common with some of the earliest forms of complex life: reptiles, amphibians, and fish. This "lizard brain" handles short-term reactions to stimuli. For example, it governs the quick withdrawal of our hand after touching a hot stove. Although necessary for our survival, the "lizard brain" is shortsighted. It is not designed to, and cannot, form links between causes and effects that are separated in time by more than a few moments. Thus it fails to register the real-life cause-and-effect relation between drinking or drugging and the consequent hangover, crash, and other damage that addiction does to our lives. It continues to associate drinking only with the cellular rush that occurs moments after ingestion. Jim suggests that we can re-educate this primitive level of our brain by sending it emotion-laden messages that associate drinking with harm and sobriety with relief. How is this done? We first review our history as addicts and "call up" the most painful moments in our drinking lives, such as, for example, when we vomited in our sleep and woke up covered in it. We distill these episodes into short slogans. Then, every morning, looking into a mirror and with our hands clasped around our solar plexus, we say our names and repeat (for example) "I do not drink or use because alcohol means vomit in my eyes." It was Jim's experience that the daily practice of these "calling up" exercises neutralized his former visceral cravings and gave him a comfortable sobriety that allows him to travel even into "dangerous territory" such as cocktail parties without the slightest twinge of temptation to use.

After almost two decades of having worked with thousands of addicted persons, Jim C. feels today that anyone who has had "the addiction experience" has sustained damage to their primitive survival system. By "getting real" about one's addiction -- both cognitively and viscerally -- on no less than a life and death emotional basis, i.e. *survival of the organism*, one can then experience a comfortable, relapse-free sobriety, free from "knee-jerk" reactions to drink or use.

Making sobriety the first priority in our lives means that we do not make our sobriety contingent on achieving a stress-free, golden-hued lifestyle.   Getting sober does allow us to get to work on problems that we had deferred while drinking, and it generally brings an improvement in the quality of our lives. But even if things go badly for us, we still maintain sobriety, no matter what.

The gist of Jim C.'s approach can be found in his "Six Suggested Guidelines for Sobriety," reprinted in the Appendix of this booklet.

2. Larry B.'s Sobriety Toolkit

Larry B., a long-time SOS convenor in the Los Angeles area, collected this kit of 47 sobriety tools. He has led four-hour SOS workshops based on the "toolkit" theme.

Did you ever try to fix or adjust something without the proper tool? These are some tools of sobriety. There are many more. Look into the population of alcoholics and the field of alcoholism and you will find a tool for whatever needs fixing or adjusting. If you don't find just the right tool, fashion one yourself.

- No matter what -- there is no valid reason on earth to drink again.

- Here's sobriety -- there's everything else -- separate and prioritize sobriety.

- Seriousness -- this is nothing less than life or death.

- Determination -- there is no turning back, especially if it gets rough. You've gotten another chance at life. How many really have that chance? Sobriety doesn't fix everything, but it makes it possible.

- Information -- retrain your brain; stimulate it with things related to alcoholism: books, audiotapes, videotapes, movies, pamphlets, brochures, meetings, plays, television and radio, newspapers and magazine articles, etc.

- People -- human contact is powerful. Try to meet people, at least one, and be sure to meet other alcoholics. Interaction fights the old patterns of isolation.

- Honesty -- this is the time to get things into the open. Get rid of the shadows and darkness of the past. Put light on the dark things and they lose their power. Things can be dealt with reasonably when they're seen as they truly are.

- Listening -- especially to people with long-term sobriety.

- Take notes -- anytime; but especially in early sobriety when memory can be tricky.

- Meetings -- be with people who want better lives and are taking actions to get what they want. Meetings are a good place to establish or reestablish social skills in a supportive environment. There is a lot to learn and feel in a meeting. You are not alone. You have not done the worst or been the most; there are always those who have "bettered" you. Think about what you hear and see, but better yet is to feel what you hear and see at meetings.

- Folk wisdom and slogans -- don't underestimate them.

- Commitments -- if you make them, keep them. You show yourself and others a lot by doing so.

- Personal "program" -- develop your own recovery process from what you hear and see. It has to be what works for you, not anybody else.

- Sharing -- surprisingly therapeutic when done honestly. Free yourself from holding things in.

- Phones -- get plenty of phone numbers of other alcoholics and use them.

- Willingness -- allow yourself to change. You have nothing to lose.

- Openness -- Don't reject ideas without at least considering them.

- Approachability -- isolation can be deadly.

- Ask questions -- no matter how foolish you think they seem. Never be afraid to ask other alcoholics about things.

- Nutrition -- improve it any way you can.

- Exercise -- however little, even just moving around.

- Help other alcoholics -- you really can keep it by giving it away.

- Joy -- it's great to be alive and sober.

- Perceptions -- it's all real, not diluted or distorted. A keen, rich mind versus a drugged, limited mind.

- Easily obtainable goals -- success breeds more success. Reach for the moon later.

- Call-up -- remember, visualize, and image behaviors and incidents from your drinking days that are repellent and associated with alcohol. Replace "alcohol good" with "alcohol bad." This is especially useful when you feel seduced by alcohol or cocksure about sobriety.

- Live in the present -- visits to the past are okay, but don't freeze your life there.

- Abstinence -- the only sure way to stay sober. Any statement to the contrary is hypothesis or commentary. Don't drink, no matter what.

- Avoid "slippery" places, people and things -- reinforce "alcohol bad" by avoiding the places, people and things you associate with "alcohol good." If you can't avoid, you must be aware that they are dangerous to your sobriety and proceed with caution.

- Safeguard your sobriety -- don't be concerned with what others think of how you do it. Don't be embarrassed if what you need to do to stay sober is "un-adult," "uncool," "weak," or "stupid" in the opinion of others. You are rebuilding and recreating yourself. You want to own your life, not be a slave to alcohol. It's your life and your sobriety. Try to avoid things like homicide and robbery as tools to keep you sober, but be as flexible as you can in using whatever it takes to safeguard your sobriety. Be aware.

- Acceptance -- of your alcoholism. Think of the things you used to do that were related to alcohol and the need to drink. Were they normal? Does anyone but an alcoholic do these things? Know that you are an alcoholic like someone with diabetes or allergies knows his or her reality. Don't be ashamed, be aware.

- Fear -- use it if you get it. Don't live in fear, but use it. The same goes for horror, shame, regret, or any other negative thoughts or feelings that may come when you think about your drinking days. Don't stifle or deny these states of mind. Use them as tools to reinforce yourself, not stumbling blocks.

- Watch for tools -- everything can be a tool to help maintain sobriety. Train your mind to see and hear tools. Don't doublethink yourself. If it works for you, use it. If you feel it may work for you, try it. You are fighting for your life, nothing less. You are the owner of your life. You are responsible for the caretaking of your life and you have decided to find better ways to live. Other people have gone before you and put together their own "tool kits." Ask them to share.

- Do it now -- procrastination is an anti-tool, feeding the negative, and working against self-esteem.

- Credit yourself -- for your attainment and maintenance of sobriety. Others may have helped, but you did it.

- Enjoy life -- you can be dead any time. Drinking is slow suicide. Life is a banquet. Depth, complexity, the full fabric of life is yours to experience. The blinders and mufflers are off. Think of yourself as a child occasionally. Experience wonder and intensity.

- It's right -- when you are sober, you feel "in your spine" that it is right. Believe your guts on this when the feeling comes.

- Care about yourself -- things you do for yourself tell you at a gut level that you care about yourself. You have the option to make things bad or good for yourself.

- Alcohol is not a tool -- everything you are able to do under alcohol's influence came from between your ears. Don't think you are less creative, a lousy dancer, etc.

- Remind yourself -- even when you think you have "got it," remind yourself. Never again. Keep it fresh.

- Imagery -- for example, be mad at alcohol. Hate it for what it has done to you and those you care about. Being free of a horrible nightmare, knowing you are sober, is far better than the relief of waking from a bad dream. You were running on empty; as your drinking progressed, you were getting closer to the end of your life.

- Make concepts real -- if you are having a bad day, start it over, anytime, any number of times.

- Visualize -- for example, drunk living is wimp living.

- Expect good things -- they happen when we expect them. Mindset in a positive light gets us to perceive positive, helpful things rather than negative, destructive things.

- Interrupt negative thoughts-- identify them as "drinking thinking" or some such. Change them, turn them around, obliterate them.

- Look at drunks -- especially when they are trying to pass as sober. Listen to what they are saying. Is that a wonderful life?

- Action -- no matter how small it seems.

Very best wishes to those who choose sobriety and life. If you really want to get and stay sober, there are people who will help you. You will be truly surprised at the lengths to which people will go to help you when you are for real.

3. Varieties of the "Daily Do" -- From the SOS Email List

The idea of doing something every day to affirm one's sobriety is a further development of the sound old idea of "one day at a time." The daily practice keeps one's commitment to sobriety fresh. SOS members use a variety of everyday "secular rituals" in their personal recovery programs. A recent survey of participants in the SOS email list (see SOS on the Internet, Appendix) gathered the following examples:

Tom Shelley: I have been fortunate to have gotten involved with a totally secular AA group from my second month of sobriety and since 1987 have been actively a part of SOS. The focus of the secular AA group (the infamous "104 Group" in St. Pete, FL) was strongly on behavior modification. Though, over the years, I have added a lot of tools to my toolbox, changing my behavior made sense then and makes sense now. The first change was, obviously, from drinking/drugging behavior to sober behavior. Then, my changes in behavior had to be oriented to maintaining this sober state. My old friend Lucybelle says "Watch the behavior," as it is the best predictor of future outcomes.

So, as many writing here have done, I make a number of daily "affirmations" of my commitment to sobriety. I note that this is a personal "choice," though the concept of "choice" is, for me, a whole 'nother issue. That aside, the other thing that I consider when discussing my sobriety, both publicly and in those many "internal dialogs" that I am prone to have is the question of whether or not I am perpetuating an "illness," or indulging in "negative thinking." Some people feel that the "need" to make a daily nod to sobriety is not only unnecessary, but counterproductive; that it somehow, and I am not sure how, keeps opening some sort of "wound" and will not allow the practitioner to get on with a normal life.

I have a lot of ways that I have found to talk about this. Among them, the fact that I consider the use of my sobriety tools, daily, akin to exercise or eating. I have to do these things to maintain my health and strength. But, today, while looking through correspondence on the Usenet "alt.recovery" groups, I ran across a quote attributed to J.R.R. Tolkien, author of the "Lord of The Rings," etc. I am going to keep this one, as it says it all, for me. Says Tolkien, "It does not pay to leave a dragon out of your calculations if you live near him." While I am loath to personify my addiction, I'll buy the metaphor.

As to what I do, I do the following. Like some others, I use this list as my starting point for the day. I begin each working day by checking my email. Almost always, there is correspondence here that deals directly with issues that affect my life. I also keep my email and refer to it often. It is the most available source of sobriety information that I have. I have been a so-called "convenor" for SOS for almost nine years. This activity keeps me actively involved in all the aspects of my "homegroup" meeting. This is not a great big deal, but it provides me with some obligations that "force" me to focus my attention on my reason for being in SOS in the first place. Using both email and the telephone, I try to make a daily contact with another sober person. This is a holdover from my AA experience and not hard to do, as I have made many friends in SOS.

I attend my regular "homegroup" meeting of

SOS on Friday nights. After the meeting I go out for food, coffee, and talk with other group members. I spend some time during my week looking for additional information on sobriety and recovery issues on the Internet, in libraries and bookstores, in newspapers, and by personal contact.

Finally, and this is not all, just what jumps to mind immediately, I talk to my family about staying sober. I have been fortunate (not a high bottom, just a big one) to have been married to the same woman for twenty-four years. Her love and help have been of inestimable value in my getting and staying sober. So, it is a natural and comfortable part of my life to share my sobriety thoughts and talk with her. And, with my daughter, Allison, who is here only by reason of the fact that I got sober and stayed sober. My sobriety is a part of all of our lives.

Aram A.: I give myself a short pep talk when I wake up every morning.

Kerrie M.: One thing that helps me stay sober is a saying I found at a Twelve-Step store. It's pasted on my bathroom mirror, so I see it every morning. The original got waterlogged, but it goes something like this, "I'd rather spend the rest of my life sober, believing I'm an alcoholic, than live it drunk or just a little bit drunk, trying to convince myself I'm not."

Rick G.: Kerrie ... I loved your "Daily Do." Reminds me of one I saw on a small desk top daily flip chart I once owned. Got it in a book store and I still see them around, if anyone likes the idea check out your local book store recovery section. I used to look forward to the morning "flip" with my coffee... I think it helped, a little bit anyway, level out the irrational b.s. going on in my head in the first few months clean and sober. I still see items like the one I described above, in my favorite book store.

Mark P.: I am a big fan of making one's living space a constant reminder for sobriety. I have several "reminders" posted about my apartment. In the kitchen I have a small "I will not be destroyed by my alcoholism." Others posted about are "The Sobriety Priority," "I don't drink no matter what." I leave some kind of recovery literature in view at all times. Jim's book is always lying about somewhere. I collect articles on recovery and there is usually one on the night stand. My bookshelf has many volumes on recovery which are visible. I have videos on recovery sitting by my VCR. It would be impossible to be in my house for more than 20 seconds without knowing that I am an alcoholic in recovery. That's the way I want it. Whatever room I am in there is something to remind my brain (lizard and otherwise) that I am in recovery.... I also check this email forum first thing every morning before I go to work. It is a nice way to start a sober day.

Larry D.: Most AA slogans made me want to puke, more so the more often I heard them. But two were really useful to me:

The first was "Easy does it!" I put a bumper sticker up high in the rear window of my jeep, the only time I was tempted to use my car as a temperance billboard, and I got some great reactions to it. I was surprised to learn how generic the slogan was; I got recognition from alcoholics, drug abusers, overeaters, gamblers, wife-abusers, and once from somebody in an organization for pedophiles in recovery. My sticker was transparent and faced outward, so when I looked in the rearview mirror the message read normally, left-to-right. Especially in my earliest days of sobriety (or was it because I was younger then?), I needed that message often, and I think the sticker helped me a lot. For sure, it saved me a few speeding tickets....

Michael O.: One of the best Xmas gifts I have received is tuning into SOS and it arrives at my computer threshold every day! Thanks to you all for being there, wherever you are.

Dudley A: I have no specific Daily Dos to remind me that drinking is not the best path for me. On the other hand, as I pack up my tennis gear for the trip to the courts every morning, I can't help but be reminded that were I still drinking (and smoking), I wouldn't be heading to the tennis courts at all. Not a bad trade-off, and my memory is such that I have no desire whatsoever to return to my less than blissful reality of yesteryear.

Ben B.: I can offhand think of three things I do on a daily basis ... that keep me sober: 1. I don't drink. 2. I don't drink. 3. Lastly, but certainly not least, I don't drink. These have been the only three things that I have consistently done every day over the last eight years. Okay, so they are all one thing. I think you get the idea.... I haven't had an urge to drink in a while, so I really don't feel the need to do any ritual around it.

4. Craig M.'s Monday Night Collection

Craig M., a Berkeley convenor, collected these 20 sobriety tips at a single Monday night Berkeley meeting, and posted them on the SOS email list.

1) Identify what physical needs alcohol met for your body. Alcohol is metabolized into water, an aldehyde, and sugar. Only sugar could satisfy a physical need/craving for your body. So maybe

you could just eat sugary foods and eliminate the alcohol middleman. I personally found that a handful of ginger cookies did most of the things for me that vodka did, without as many bad side effects. It made quitting easier.

2) Keep busy. Sign up for a class, take on a big project at work, start a new hobby, build a boat in the basement. It helps a lot if your new activities keep you out of the house during any times of the day you used to regularly drink heavily.

3) Exercise. Walk or bike to work, or walk over lunch.

4) Always have safe beverages nearby. If you become hooked on diet Pepsi or Dr. Pepper, you aren't going to suffer nearly the same consequences as from being addicted to alcohol. The group split pretty much evenly on the issue of non-alcoholic beer, some finding it valuable and safe while others view it as so dangerous that "drinking even one NA beer would be a relapse." Know yourself and your limits.

5) Get alcoholic hepatitis or pancreatitis — there's nothing like physical pain and the knowledge that you'll die if you start drinking again to keep you sober during those challenging first months of sobriety. Obviously I'm just kidding on this point, but finding out you are really seriously sick can be a strong motivator.

6) Stay away from parties for a while. It doesn't have to be permanent, but make it easier for yourself at first. If you do go to parties, go with your family or stick close to home so you can easily leave if you get uncomfortable.

7) Be kind to yourself. Use "discomfort with alcohol" as an excuse to skip those boring family events you dread for completely unrelated rea-

sons. Get a massage, sleep in on the weekend, treat yourself to something you want but wouldn't normally get.

8) Think of sobriety as a possibly temporary thing during the first few months, when things are hard. This may sound dangerous, but it's not that different than the "one day at a time" approach that some people use.

9) Remember your hangovers, dry heaves, arrests, and other negative consequences. Keep these memories fresh.

10) Do everything in tiny little steps. Don't jump back to your "normal" patterns too quickly.

11) Examine your alcohol-substitute behaviors, to make sure they aren't potentially a problem.

12) Remind yourself that you "aren't going to be happy with just one drink, so why have it?" when the thought that "just one wouldn't hurt" pops into your head.

13) No alcohol in the house. Absolutely. If guests bring it to a dinner or party, make them leave it in the car.

14) Remember that everyone is an individual, and what works for others might not work for you. There is no one true way.

15) Identify situations where you drank in the past, and try to see what it was about them that led you to drink to excess. If you have relapsed, examine everything about it to try to learn what the problem was. Ask others for their feedback, since you might be blind to something about yourself which is obvious to everyone else.

16) You don't need alcohol to sleep. Alcohol *causes* sleep pattern problems. It might be hard for a week or two, but after a while you will sleep better than ever before.   My own decades-long

insomnia has completely vanished. Remember, it may take six months to completely return to your normal sleep patterns, so be patient.

17) Watch out for danger times — be especially vigilant when you are angry, having a hard time being productive, etc.

18) Try meditation.

19) Immerse yourself in recovery — read a lot of books, go to tons of meetings. Take on a leadership role in your recovery meetings. (That has the benefit of making it somewhat mandatory to go to the meetings.)

20) Be open to introspection. The key to success is the ability to take an honest look at ourselves. You have to change some pretty deeply ingrained patterns, and you can't do it on autopilot.

Posted on SOS Email List 4/26/97

5. Marty's N.'s One-Two-Three

Marty N., an Oakland/Berkeley convenor, posted this personal testimonial to the SOS email list on his fourth sobriety anniversary.

Four years ago yesterday I had my last drink. Today, on the fourth anniversary of my sobriety, my wife and two boys and I went out after soccer practice to a local Mexican restaurant and celebrated with lemonades and root beers. Afterwards I cleaned my toolbox in the garage, and then read my youngest a portion of *The White Seal* by Kipling for bedtime. Now my wife is correcting her Oakland third graders' reading homework, and I'm in bed next to her trying to put the how and why of my sobriety down on my laptop.

I had a lot of help and support getting here. My boys, especially the oldest, helped to get me across the threshold of Kaiser to seek help, and have been enthusiastic supporters of my sobriety all along. My wife and I went through some very rocky times along around year 2 and part of 3, but we have come out on the other side. She considers my sobriety the biggest gift she could have had, and from her I hear a series of stories about other marriages where the man drinks and maybe also abuses the wife and kids, and all the problems they have, that we don't, thanks to my sobriety. She makes me feel good.

My biggest debt, though, is to SOS. SOS showed me the basic human respect of not presuming to know all my problems in advance and of not having a ready-made formula to fix me up. Instead of trying to sell me a panacea or recruit me into a cult, SOS laid back and let me find my own feet. With a cunning that it took me years to discover and to appreciate, SOS understood that the only program for recovery that works for you is the one you fashion for yourself because you really want it. SOS for me has not been a ready-made off-the-shelf treatment program, but rather a safe and rich environment in which I could devise a treatment for my own self. Safe, because I have learned in these meetings that no matter what I say and reveal about my inner hurts, no harm will come to me. Rich, because by listening to the other participants and reading the literature, I have available to me a wealth of insights, tools and methods for overcoming my enemy within, and for leading a sober life.

It probably took me six months of going to two SOS meetings a week, and going to four or five Kaiser meetings on top of it, before the coin dropped in my head and I "got" the fact that I was

an alcoholic. Prior to that time I had believed that
to be an alcoholic was to be a bad person, or a
moral weakling; and this impression was rein-
forced by my peripheral acquaintance with the
literature of AA, with its emphasis on "character
defects" and its rituals of blame and shame. As
long as this was my concept, I knew I was not an
alcoholic, because I knew that I was not a bad
person and that I was not a moral weakling, or
lacking in will or resolution of character. What I
finally got clear is that I was organically dam-
aged, either by heredity or by acquisition, and
that my body did not process alcohol the same
way as normal people did. My body lacks the
"stop" switch that naturally and without effort of
will quenches normal people's desire to drink as
their blood alcohol levels rise. That limiting cir-
cuit is absent or broken in my system. As a
consequence, I can never safely drink again.
Although I am liable to clean up the messes I
made while drunk, like anyone else, I am as
blameless for my inability to control my intake as
incontinents are for their inability to control their
output. We just don't have the mechanism.

Around the time I came to this realization, I
had a client who suffered from Duchene's syn-
drome (muscular dystrophy); he was wheelchair
bound, unable to control his functions, and most
of his bones stuck under his skin at odd angles.
Yet, though he could barely write and could not
keep his head up for long, he had a clarity of
mind and a ferocity of spirit that all who knew
him admired. In the brief contact we had before
he succumbed, I came to see that the disability of
the sober alcoholic is a feather-light cross to bear,
by comparison. All that we cannot do in our lives
is drink alcohol or use drugs. How many would
gladly trade their disability for ours!

Once I "got it," once I understood and accepted that I was an alcoholic, the rest came easier. Over the course of the following months, I pieced together for myself a self-treatment program that perfectly suits my individual history and situation. I would like to share it, in a few words, with others on this list, by way of passing along some of the helpful points that others passed down to me.

Number one, I try to do something every day to remind myself that I am an alcoholic and cannot drink or use, no matter what. Jim C. makes a big point of this in all his writings, and his Triumph workshop constitutes the nuclear-strength version of such an everyday denial-buster. (We also have the Journal of Sobriety for those who like to work with pens and pencils.) At first it was drinking decaf in the morning, instead of caf, that reminded me. Then I started taking B-complex vitamins to restore my depleted body chemistry, and swallowing those horse-sized pills every morning definitely jogged my brain. Moreover, the vitamins turned my urine neon-yellow, so that the reminder repeated itself throughout the day. Then I mentally associated tooth brushing with affirming my alcoholism, and that worked for a time. Lately I've been using my participation in this email list as my Daily Do. A few months ago my wife took a weight reduction class, and the instructor there, in a very similar vein, gave them a long list of healthy eating practices and told them they had to do Something Of Something ("SOS") every day. So, having an everyday ritual of affirmation, a daily denial of denial, is a very "SOS" thing to do.

Number two, I try to participate regularly and actively in SOS meetings. Fortunately our meetings are small enough where you cannot sit behind a pole and daydream. This was hard for me at first, as I was not accustomed to revealing feelings or speaking about myself in meetings, and I resisted it. Even after four years it sometimes takes me nearly the whole meeting before I can open up inside and share. One of my Kaiser counselors, Dr. Boyd, pointed out once that our feelings are one of the few things in life that we can change by merely talking about them, and this is true for me. If I am feeling lonely or depressed, or stressed, or ashamed, or guilty, I can unload the poison from those feelings by sharing them with the group. This helps to relieve emotional stresses that might drive me to drinking. Sometimes just saying "Hi, I'm Marty, I'm an alcoholic" in front of my friends at the SOS meeting is all that I need to do. Often it's the things that come out of my mouth unsuspected that help me change, more than the things that come into my ears. Participation in meetings also helps me regain basic social and psychological skills, stunted during years where the bottle was my best and only "friend." Active participation strengthens my ability to empathize with others, and my ability to ride out and accept my own feelings without panicking and reaching for an anaesthetic. Participation in SOS meetings has helped me not only to stay sober, but also to recover from the damage I did myself during my three decades of active alcoholism.

Three, I've discovered for myself that the famous Sobriety Priority is a useful way to analyze what I do in life. As Jim C. has written so many times, we prioritize sobriety as a separate issue so that we do not drink or use, no matter what. When I drank, almost everything I did had drinking connected to it as a separate issue. Now that I am sober, almost everything is related somehow to sobriety. I can view the flowchart of my life as a series of decisions, some of whose branches tend to lead toward sobriety and others toward relapse. Even tiny decisions, such as whether to look at a highway beer billboard, can involve a battle between my sober self and the addict within me for control of my eye muscle. Which conduct is correct? The Sobriety Priority is a bright line through the blooming, buzzing confusion of life. There are a few days when I find my brain doing this kind of analysis, applying the Sobriety Priority, hundreds of times. You might be amazed at the kind of problems the Sobriety Priority algorithm can analyze and solve.

Taken together, my One, Two, and Three form a closely-knit matrix of support for my sober life. Both my mind and my feelings are engaged. My personal program involves both my inner and my outer relations. There's something sober I do twice weekly, something sober I do daily, and something sober I can do anytime or all the time. So, as near as I can figure it out, that's how I've managed, after thirty plus years of drinking, to get sober and stay sober for four.

(Posted on the SOS Email List 10/2/96)

Concluding Thoughts

Sobriety is what we make it. We can master our addiction by our own efforts, and with a little help from our sober friends. Sobriety is no more a gift from a deity than addiction is a curse of devils. The power to be a sober person lies within each of us. Instead of surrendering and ceasing to think, as some urge us, we need to become proactive and think harder and better. Instead of "letting go" we need to "pick up" the various sobriety tools and try them out.

Here's a suggestion to get started. Take a blank

sheet of paper and write at the top: "My Sobriety Program." Then draw a vertical line down the middle. Caption the left column: "Problem." Caption the right column: "Tool to Try." Fill in the left column with specific facts. For example: "Crave to drink at happy hour." Or: "Can I make it through office party?" Or: "Depressed!" List as many as occur to you. Then start sketching in the right side column ... you get the idea. You've started building your sobriety program. On paper or mentally, keep revising and revising until you get it working right. If you fail, pick yourself up and start again. Every sober day is a victory, and the credit is yours.

As we put sober days end to end, we gather confidence in our ability. Before long, we come to prefer our sober lifestyle. We can hold up our head again; we can feel our feelings again; we can pay our bills; hold our job; we can look life in the eye. We work to protect our sobriety. We may be filled with warmth and gratitude to those who have helped us. And one of the things we may want to do is to make sobriety more readily available to others by taking a more active role in SOS meetings.

CHAPTER FIVE
THE CARE AND FEEDING
OF SOS MEETINGS

If a meeting is to work well for its members as a place to build their sobriety, we need to pay careful attention to the way the meeting is set up and operated. Leadership roles, meeting format, and finances are three points that require particular attention. You have complete autonomy in SOS how you structure your meeting, so long as you stay on the three common foundations of secularity, sobriety, and self-help. This chapter contains some ideas and examples drawn from actual ongoing meetings, which you can use for suggestion and inspiration.

[A] Leadership

There was heavy rain at a recent Friday night meeting, and the meeting secretary, who traveled by bicycle, was definitely going to be late. He had the only copy of the opening statement with him. No matter: at a few minutes after the hour, the members collectively pieced the opening statement together from memory, and the meeting began. Nearly everyone present was a leader, and any one of them could have opened, led, and closed the meeting. The more there are who can do this, the stronger the meeting. A meeting where only one or two can lead is fragile, weak.

Typically, the meeting defines two or more leadership roles that rotate among the members. The most essential roles are those of secretary and of treasurer.

The **secretary** (also often called convenor) would typically include in his or her job description the following: arrive a few minutes early to open up, turn on the lights, arrange the room, set up the literature, bring the opening statement and the signup list, read or get someone to read the opening statement, keep the discussion on the foundations if necessary, deal with problem situations as required, pass around and collect the signup sheet if one is used, sign attendance slips if required, keep an eye on the clock, and bring the meeting to a close.

The secretary also has duties outside the meeting. The secretary keeps the SOS Clearinghouse and the Internet web sites informed of the current meeting place, time, contact phone number, and other relevant information. The Clearinghouse telephone number is 310-821-8430; fax 310-821-2610. The SOS Internet Home Page in San Francisco is at www.unhooked.com. See the Appendix for more detailed information. The secretary also attends and represents the meeting at intergroup functions.

Some meeting secretaries do much more: they may telephone members who are unexpectedly absent to see if they have an emergency and need help; they may organize special meeting events such as movies, book nights, or social gatherings; they print and post flyers, place public service ads, talk to counselors or groups about SOS, publish or write for the national or local newsletters and web sites, participate in the SOS email list, maintain the voicemail or message machine for the group's contact telephone number, etc. Or your meeting may wish to divide up these responsibilities among several members.

The **treasurer** is necessary because the organization has expenses and needs to collect funds. Most meeting sites charge rent. Flyers, literature, telephone lines, Yellow Pages listings, social events, newsletters, and other goods and services the meeting or group of meetings deems essential must all be supported out of local funds. A share of the meeting's revenue needs to go as regularly and consistently as possible toward the support of the Clearinghouse. How large a share is up to the meeting; a reasonable range is 10-25 per cent.

Elect as treasurer someone who is a regular with the group, who is financially stable, and whose home address is known to group members. The treasurer typically keeps a basket, a book, and the funds. The treasurer passes the basket; a good time is when everyone has arrived at the meeting who is expected to arrive. At the end of the meeting the treasurer tallies the contents, and records the amount in the book. It is a good idea also to record the amount on the meeting signup sheet, if used, as a backup. The treasurer forwards the meeting's contribution to the SOS Clearinghouse, pays the meeting rent and whatever other expenditures the meeting has decided, and makes a financial report to the group at business meetings, usually each month. The treasurer also attends intergroup functions and represents the meeting there. The treasurer's job also should rotate as much as practical.

You may also want to have:

- a librarian, responsible for getting and distributing sobriety books, pamphlets, flyers, meeting schedules, and other material, and perhaps for leading group discussion based on reading material;
- a publicity person, responsible for out-

reach, placing ads, etc.;

- a refreshment coordinator;

- a new member secretary, responsible for following up with new members to make sure their questions are answered and concerns addressed;

- a speakers' bureau, to train members in giving public appearances on behalf of SOS before clinics, schools, other meetings, or wherever invited;

- a steering committee, to combine the various service functions. Or you may want to divide these functions among several people.

Leadership is a necessary service to the group. People who have performed these services testify that doing so helps their recovery. Doing service work strengthens their sober identity, helps them to feel good about being sober, and motivates them to do more. The opportunity to render leadership services needs to be shared as widely as possible among the regular group participants.

Leadership can also have its negative side. Leaders may come to feel after a time that they are better, wiser, stronger, or smarter than others, and may begin to pose as gurus, amateur therapists, or other authorities over the members. That kind of "leadership" is a departure from the self-help foundation of SOS. Regular rotation of leadership positions, perhaps at six month intervals, helps to keep this kind of corruption from developing.

At this time, SOS does not have an equivalent for the role of "sponsor" in AA. AA meetings were originally secret and you could only find one if you were invited. The person who invited you and introduced you was your "sponsor." That kind of sponsor is no longer necessary now that meetings are publicized. AA nevertheless has retained the sponsor role but in a new form. The contemporary sponsor is like a doctor, priest, lawyer, and trustee all rolled into one, but without any diploma, license, malpractice insurance, bond, or review board. It is a powerful role rife with possibilities for abuse. SOS has shied away from investing anyone with that much power over another member, on basic democratic, self-help, and safety principles. However, new members who want more individual contact and personal involvement can and do attach themselves informally to older members and make friends and/or mentors of them. Periodically there are discussions in SOS whether to formalize these relationships, but this remains for the future, if at all.

There is no hard and fast rule about how much sober time a candidate should have before being elected to leadership. A good rule of thumb is six months sober in SOS, but in some situations candidates with less time have served very successfully. More important than counting months is whether the individual has the respect of the other members, understands and is committed to the SOS way of doing things, and is motivated to serve.

Elections to leadership in ongoing meetings are usually by consensus. Elections will not be very useful if they are held by surprise, or without preparation, or if two camps form, or if less than the full membership is present, or if the voting is secret. Elections are most useful if they are announced in advance, if volunteers are sought or nominated in advance, if there is already consensus, and if the full membership of the meeting is there to vote by a simple show of hands with the candidates present. There are no speeches. Usually SOS elections are simple, trouble-free affairs that occupy at most a few minutes of the meeting's time.

[B] Opening Statement.

The opening statement is a useful ritual that signals the formal beginning of the meeting. It informs newcomers and reminds old-timers of the basic purpose of the group. It outlines the format and ground rules of the meeting. It gets the ball rolling. Usually the meeting secretary reads the statement or asks for a volunteer to read it.

Each meeting is free to compose its own opening statement, provided the contents are consistent with the basic purposes of SOS. Drafting or revising an opening statement might be a good process for the members of a new group to go through as part of their self-help activity. Several sample opening statements from different SOS groups around the country are given in the Appendix for reference. Opening statements should not go on too long. Note that all opening statements refer in some manner to the three foundations of SOS: we are secular, we define sobriety as abstinence from alcohol and drugs, and we are a self-help organization. The opening also serves to remind people that the contents of the meeting are confidential, that you must be sober to participate, and perhaps also that you should respect other people's time by not monopolizing the floor.

Directly after the reading of the opening statement, many meetings allow for introductions, especially of newcomers. Newcomers may be invited to state their first name and to say a few words about themselves. Then everyone in the meeting will do likewise in response.

Announcements and time for special concerns usually follow directly after introductions. Announcements include special meetings or social events, and other business items. Members will sometimes announce here that they plan to be absent at the next meeting for vacation or some other reason. "Special concerns" is a broad category that allows members to put on the meeting's agenda important events in their lives during the past week. Members here share such events as sobriety anniversaries, relapses, job losses or promotions, graduations, marriages, births, deaths, injuries, and the like. In some cases, the concern turns into the main topic of the meeting; in others, it passes without comment.

After announcements and special concerns comes the main part of the meeting. How this is handled varies from meeting to meeting. Some meetings simply go to open discussion with no definite theme. Others use the "chair" system with a defined topic, or focus the discussion on selected readings passed out in advance. Some allow crosstalk during the whole meeting; others only in part of the meeting, or not at all. Below are some of the points you may want to consider when deciding which format to use.

[C] Sharing and Crosstalk

"Sharing" has a very definite meaning in self-help groups. It means that the person recounts their experience and thoughts, without expecting response or comment of any sort. Sharing is an exclusively one-way form of communication. It is a monologue. In technical terms, it is a half-duplex connection. The person talks, everybody else listens. Then the next person talks, and everybody else listens. Then the next. At no point is anyone's "share" an answer or other direct response to anyone else's. Each share stands entirely on its own, complete and sufficient unto itself.

"Crosstalk" means two-way communication, dialogue, a full-duplex connection. In crosstalk, a person expects a response and may respond in turn, creating a conversation. A third may join in, and more, until everybody is chattering away like birds in spring.

Although crosstalk feels more natural and may appear to be more therapeutic, many contend that the real work in self-help groups is done during sharing time. The "no response" rule of sharing time protects the speaker from having their statement judged, criticized, ridiculed, or otherwise attacked. This in turn promotes the fullest possible openness and honesty, qualities that are essential to self-change. When sharing is at its best, speakers will find themselves saying things they did not consciously plan, but which came out of their mouths from some inner concern of which they were unaware; and these can be powerful moments of self-revelation and self-acceptance, secular epiphanies where transformation is visible in the person's countenance and bearing. These times when the self-help process is visibly at work are precious, awesome moments in a group's life.

But there are also canned, boring shares, rehearsed "drunkalogues" that amount to mere bragging and one-downs-manship. If your sharing time consists mostly of this sort of speech-making, consider dissolving the meeting. One of the beauties of SOS is the prevalence of "soberlogues" that address life in the sober present rather than dwelling in the past.

Crosstalk wants to be handled with great care, respect, and humor. We in recovery have typically gone through great pain, self-loathing, guilt, shame, rage, and a mess of other feelings. We may be raw, edgy, hair-trigger, exceedingly timid, suicidal, murderous, or deeply depressed, or a combination of all the above. So, rudeness, sarcasm and thoughtlessness are not appreciated; preaching and unasked advice will quickly make enemies; and even ordinary innocent curiosity may deeply threaten or offend someone. The most valued qualities in crosstalk are kindness, sincerity, tact, and above all humor. The member who can make the group laugh is always a valued crosstalk participant.

Sharing and crosstalk both have their place. Many meetings allot three fourths of the main meeting time to sharing, one fourth to crosstalk. What you do in your meeting is up to you.

[D] Chair and Topic

During the main part of your meeting, discussion may be completely at random, or you may try to organize it around a topic. If you use the topic system, you will want a person to introduce the topic and get the talk rolling. That person is usually called a chairperson or just "chair" but may be called "speaker" or something else. Since chairs are best designated in advance, you will also need a signup list for them, and the secretary or someone else will need to circulate this and make sure that a volunteer for the next meeting has come forward. You will need a fallback procedure for those weeks when the designated chair is unexpectedly absent. Some meetings make this their "round-robin" night when everyone talks in turn about their personal recovery program.

The chair's duty is to select a topic and introduce it. No special qualification or length of sobriety is required to be chair. It is an excellent task for persons early in sobriety. Selecting a topic may occupy the chairperson's mind with sobriety thoughts daily or hourly for the week before the meeting, which is very therapeutic. Introducing the topic with a few minutes' talk is a good way to learn the skill of sharing. The chair may also conduct the meeting during sharing time, taking over temporarily from the secretary, and thus can practice meeting leadership skills, with the secretary available as a backup.

The chair & topic system is meant to rotate the chair each week and give everyone a turn at setting the topic. In this way, every participant has their concern aired by the whole meeting periodically, ensuring that meetings don't become monopolized by the interests of one or a handful of talkative individuals.

If you use the chair & topic system, why not keep a record of the topic? Make a space on the signup sheet for it. That way after a while you'll have a treasure trove of topics to consult, which can help chairpersons who are searching, and can call up memories of outstanding meetings for you. One such list compiled from two meetings is attached in the Appendix.

The chair & topic system is not meant to be a rigid mold. If you have nothing to share on the evening's topic, but have something entirely different on your mind, by all means share that. It often takes just a little stretching, and can be a source of general merriment, to "relate" your concern to the topic, no matter how improbably.

[E] Signup Sheet

Many but not all meetings make use of a signup sheet. A sample signup sheet is given in the Appendix. Signing the sheet and giving your phone number is always optional, and the general practice is to use first names and last initials only. The sheet has several purposes. By signing and putting your telephone number on the list, you give permission to another member to call you if they need help. The secretary can use the signup sheet as a record of meeting attendance over time. The sheet also helps the members get to know each others' names, and serves as a way of affirming their sobriety psychologically by "signing in" to the meeting. The secretary circulates, collects, and preserves the signup sheets. On occasion, secretaries have used the signup sheets to do a telephone survey of past meeting participants to find out their reactions to the program and their success at staying sober. If this is done tactfully and with respect for the respondents' privacy, it can be an educational process. Such a survey done in Atlanta showed that every past participant, without exception, was still sober.

[F] Closing

SOS meetings do not include prayer or other religious observances. Therefore, the custom prevalent in AA meetings of ending with the Lord's Prayer would be completely out of place in an SOS meeting. Most meetings end without any sort of ceremony. The secretary merely seizes on the appropriate moment to state that it's time to go. Some meetings hold hands at the end and wish each other a sober week. A happy ceremony that some meetings practice is to give each other, at the end, a round of applause for having stayed sober another week.

Some meetings make it a custom to go out for refreshments after the meeting. This promotes friendship among the members and gives the meeting a stronger sense of community. This seems desirable, since that is essentially what SOS is: a secular self-help community.

As you progress in your SOS sobriety, you may have occasion to wish that more people had the opportunity to attend SOS meetings. Or you may find yourself hatching an idea for an SOS meeting that serves a special need or a distinct population, or that uses a different format or structure than your regular meeting. Or you may be reading this in a town where there is no SOS meeting at all, and you are thinking about starting the very first one. If so, the following chapter is especially for you.

CHAPTER SIX
HOW TO START AN SOS MEETING

Even with no help and limited resources, starting a group is not difficult. The only true requirement for starting an SOS meeting is the honest desire to do so and the energy to make that desire real. You can set up a time and place to meet, publicize that information, and then be there. If only one other person shows up, you can have a meeting. It is easier, however, if you have a few people interested before you begin. And it will be a fortunate thing for your group if several of these persons have some self-help experience. Any background in other groups is very helpful, especially if that encounter included some time in recovery.

There are a number of meetings that have been established over the last ten years. The experience gained by those who started these meetings has been collected and distilled into the accompanying suggestions. Please consider these items carefully: they are the result of hundreds, if not thousands of hours of work. No need to re-invent the wheel.

[1] Starting Up

The Meeting Place

You will need to settle on a place to meet. In some cases, SOSers have started meetings in their homes. If your community is very small or there is no way that you can do otherwise, go ahead. But most people will find a public meeting place is preferable. Additionally, if you try to have meetings in a member's home or in any other place owned or controlled by a member, you may encounter proprietary problems. If that is all you have at the beginning, you may have to make do with it. But consider rental of a neutral place as soon as possible.

A meeting place can be just about anywhere, but it is more likely that you will attract others to the meeting if it is held in a relatively convenient, comfortable, and safe place. Many places recommend themselves as meeting places for SOS. Places that may have meeting spaces available include libraries, schools, colleges and universities, hospitals, community parks and recreation centers, banks, public utilities, union halls, and even churches, so long as the separation of SOS and the church is clear. For instance, the church may have a separate building or community hall available.

Choose according to your size and financial ability. Whatever you do, tell the owner ahead of time the purpose of your group and the fact that it is secular in nature. Do all you can to avoid any possible future misunderstanding that might surprise anyone and cause disruption to your meeting.

You should base your choice on your own best judgment as to the needs of your proposed group. If funds are scarce, and no doubt they will be, suggest to your potential landlord a payment of a percentage of your meeting's collection. But, if other arrangements cannot be made, accepting space, gratis, is preferable to not having a meeting place at all. Even if a meeting place is offered to you at no charge, a small payment towards electricity and other expenses is always appreciated.

By doing this, you maintain group autonomy, avoid possible conflicts, and enhance group esteem.

The Meeting Time and Length

Once you have a place to meet, the next step is to determine when you meet and for how long. Again, the choice is entirely up to those in your group. Having a meeting one evening a week is the usual pattern. You may have to experiment to find which day and time are best. There are successful meetings at breakfast time, lunch, mid-afternoon, and other time slots.

Pick what YOU need. Meetings traditionally last from an hour to an hour and a half. Again, try to think what will work, and change it later if you need to. Whatever you finally decide upon, try to be consistent. This last point is important. Once you establish a meeting time and place, be there, rain or shine.

The Group Name

Many SOS groups distinguish themselves by choosing a name. The name can be anything that you think will help you and others identify your affiliation and purpose. It can be as simple as, "The Tuesday Nite SOS Group", or as lengthy as, "The Northwest, Lunchtime, Secular Organizations for Sobriety Support for Addictions, Abstinence, and Freedom from Chemical Dependency." Use what you think will suit you best. As the group begins to form, you may wish to change the name to better reflect your collective goals, or orientation.

As SOS is our most well-recognized acronym, you may wish to include that. If you are able to get listings in the phone book, or other alphabetized guides, if you start them with "SOS" you will make it easier for others to find your listing.

Finding Allies

At the outset, and perhaps for some time, you may find yourself sitting in an empty meeting place week after week with a diminishing sense of expectation that anyone will ever join you. Don't worry, it happens everywhere and is only natural. There are a number of steps you can take to minimize your lonely wait.

You can begin by understanding the reason you are there. Starting a meeting and attending it with regularity is an active and strong affirmation of your sobriety. The benefits derived from meeting attendance are many: camaraderie, sharing of experience, a sense of belonging, to name but a few. But first and foremost is the fact that you have made a strong behavioral statement for you and your sobriety. The importance of this cannot be emphasized too strongly, but, at times, in the absence of other meeting participants, the importance may begin to pale.

The task of establishing a meeting by yourself can be daunting. Many convenors have lightened that burden and given their meetings a headstart by finding an ally. An ally is another person who shares your value in staying sober, in a secular manner, and is as willing as you to devote some of their time and energy to getting the meeting going. If you have spent any time discussing forming an SOS meeting with other sober friends, consider asking them to be a part of it, now, if you haven't already.

Finding yourself an ally prior to starting a meeting has the added benefit of allowing you to find out how receptive your area is to having an

SOS presence. Additionally, having an ally will enable you to share the legwork necessary to getting your meeting off the ground. And, of course, come meeting time, you won't be sitting there alone. Your meeting will already have two members (or more, if you're lucky).

How to find an ally is up to you, but here are a few suggestions. Many come to SOS from other recovery organizations, AA, etc. If this describes you then it is likely you are not the only one in your area who feels a need for a change. Look to the groups that you already attend or have attended in the past. Listen to what people are saying. You will find those of like mind if you just dig a bit. If you are acquainted with a chemical dependency counselor, perhaps they can put you in touch with others they know who are looking for an alternative to the common support groups. You might try an ad in the local newspaper classified under the "personals" or "counseling and support" areas.

[2] PROMOTION

People are not accustomed to looking for secular support groups! Most secular people in need seem to have either settled, with resignation, for groups with religious overtones or have given up trying to find any help at all from existing groups and institutions. You have to let these people know where you are and what you are doing.

Be ready to invest some time, energy, and perhaps a little money. What you do will likely have to be repeated over and over again until word of mouth begins to take effect. When SOS is as well known as AA, we can relax a little on promotion! Meanwhile, you can try these strategies:

* Contact the SOS Clearinghouse, by mail, fax, or telephone. The address is 5521 Grosvenor Boulevard, Los Angeles, CA 90066. The phone number is 310-821-8430; fax 310-821-2610. Let them know all the particulars about your meeting. Among the most important things you can consider doing is making the information about your meeting as public as possible. You can do this by allowing the meeting information to be posted on one of the SOS World Wide Web sites on the Internet. The SOS Home Page in the San Francisco Bay Area at **www.unhooked.com** tries to maintain an up-to-date and complete worldwide SOS meeting list. For topics of particular interest to meeting convenors, log on to the SOS Convenors' Page at http://home1.gte.net/markp/index.htm with your browser.

* Mail a press release to local radio stations, both AM and FM. Address them to the Program Director or Public Service Director. See sample press release in the Appendix.

* Mail a press release to the newspapers, daily and weekly. Address them to the Editorial Department. If you know that a paper has a community calendar, mail a press release to that department for a possible listing.

* Mail a press release and a bulletin board announcement to any local cable television companies in your community. Many cable companies will run this kind of announcement on the local access channel on a continuing basis.

* Make extensive use of bulletin boards in laundromats, food markets, gyms, hospitals, schools, colleges, senior citizen centers, neighborhood centers, etc. See the sample flyer in the Appendix.

* Contact local "throw-away" free papers. Some

of these may run regular SOS meeting announcement listings in their "on-going groups" section at no charge. Find out what their requirements are and make use of this free listing.

* Make up, or have printed, business cards which have your name and phone number, along with the time, day, and location of your meeting. Place these cards anywhere that you think interested people may find them. One strategy employed by some SOSers is to place a card in each and every book about alcoholism, treatment, addiction, etc. in the local libraries and bookstores. This is called "salting." It is an effective method and tends to attract a number of people.

* Let the local alcohol/drug dependency treatment community know about your new group. A large proportion of our inquiry phone calls are from professionals in the area who want to be able to refer people in treatment to secular support meetings. A simple postcard with the name, location, and time of your meeting, along with a local contact telephone number, can be sent to hospital alcohol units; private treatment facilities; city, county, and state facilities; and individual therapists who specialize in drug dependency treatment. This can be very effective. See sample letter in the Appendix.

The suggestions here are very basic in nature, and you will probably think of other good ways to reach those who need SOS. As your group develops, you will have help in getting the word out. It will, no doubt, take a while before you see meaningful results. Stick with it and try to be patient — it is important to not let yourself become overwhelmed.

Here is a real life example of how one convenor built a successful SOS campus meeting. Laura L.

contributed this to the SOS email list in response to a request for the "gory details" about how the meeting became a recognized campus institution. She wrote:

When I realized that our group "leader" was no longer interested in any meeting, SOS or otherwise, I offered to "take the reins" over. Here's what I did.

- Called the place where we were sometimes holding our meeting and got the official OK to meet there. It had been a verbal OK from someone she knew who worked there. Got a schedule for a year's worth of meetings, and they agreed that, since this is a needed public service, no rent was due. Discontinued the practice of meeting at a local cafeteria where nobody new would want to go looking for us.

- Called the local newspaper to find out who to communicate with for inclusion in the "Support Groups" section of the community calendar. They said mail it in to George H. Mailed it. Mailed it again. Mailed it again and again. Got pissed 'cause they weren't printing it. Called George. George advised me to fax it. I faxed it. I began faxing it every week and making a general pain in the ass of myself. They seemed to get the message.

- Got 50 each of the four SOS "pamphlets" from the Clearinghouse.

- Started passing the hat at meetings; we had never done this under the "old" leader.

- With monies collected, began building a group "library." We now have about 15 books and some audio tapes, mostly on alcoholism/addiction but also on other issues, such as ACOA, men's issues, women's issues, etc. I also turn over my copy of "Sobering Thoughts" from Women for Sobriety (WFS) to the meeting.

- Wrote a short letter to all of the local "resource centers" letting them know who we are, what we do, etc. I might add that all of these groups call me annually to make sure that everything is still the same. I've gotten several referrals from these folks: alcoholics as well as addicts.

- Oh no! Lost our meeting space after a year! I think that the AA group that met at the hospital had something to do with that ... they still meet there, but we were told that there was no more room.

- Began "agitating" at school through the student health service for meeting space. University rules say that extra-scholastic activities must be sponsored. Mailed lengthy letter and brochures to Head Honcho of student mental health office. Nice guy. Of course he'll sponsor us, and by the way, he'd like to meet with me.

- New place is a palace.

- Called George again about the change in meeting place. Called again. Cut my losses and began another fax campaign of terror. He got the message.

- Plastered entire university with posters that have two inverted wine glasses or two crossed hypodermic syringes and the caption, "Had enough? If you're having trouble with alcohol or drugs, why not join us for a meeting."

- Delivered 50 card versions of the poster to

student health services. They were placed in waiting rooms and exam rooms. Also in the counseling and testing center.

- I make it a point to call Head Honcho at mental health regularly and let him know how we are doing, and more importantly, how much we appreciate the university's support. Support breeds support.
- I tenaciously promote "my" group. I do not miss meetings. I make newcomers welcome. If they take a book on loan and we never see them again, at least I have planted the seed. I start meetings on time. I try to live an example. I try to let people see, like Tom the listmeister showed me long ago, that you can be sober and still laugh a lot.

That's it. If I think of anything else (heaven help us all!) I'll let you know.

Appendix

Notes

Suggested Guidelines for Sobriety

To break the cycle of denial and achieve sobriety, we first acknowledge that we are alcoholics or addicts.

We reaffirm this truth daily and accept without reservation the fact that as clean and sober individuals, we can not and do not drink or use, no matter what.

Since drinking or using is not an option for us, we take whatever steps are necessary to continue our Sobriety Priority lifelong.

A quality of life, "the good life," can be achieved. However, life is also filled with uncertainties. Therefore, we do not drink or use regardless of feelings, circumstances, or conflicts.

We share in confidence with each other our thoughts and feelings as sober, clean individuals.

Sobriety is our Priority, and we are each responsible for our lives and sobriety.

From *How To Stay Sober*, by James Christopher (1988).

Suggested Guidelines for Family and Friends

Be gentle with yourself and the alcoholic/addict in your family. Remember, sobriety skills are not developed overnight, so give yourself credit for being understanding.

Attend as many SOS meetings as you can. If you like, attend other family recovery group meetings. Take what you can use from these and leave the rest.

Get names and phone numbers from sober alcoholics/addicts and their family members at meetings. Use these phone numbers. Practice calling people when you are feeling OK so that you will be able to call more easily when you are in need of help.

Try putting some simplified structure into your life: get up and get dressed at a regular time, take a walk before or after dinner, etc.

Do some reading on alcoholism and addiction from the books on the Recommended Reading List. Visit a local library or bookstore and see what others they may have to offer.

Sample Opening Statements

From Oakland/Berkeley, California:

This is a regular open meeting of SOS, Secular Organizations for Sobriety / Save Our Selves, Oakland/Berkeley Meeting. We are a support group for people who want to get sober and stay sober. We call ourselves "secular" because we make no use of religious concepts in our efforts to remain clean and sober. We believe that in order to recover we must make sobriety the top priority in our lives. By sobriety we mean total abstinence from alcohol and other mood-altering drugs. The primary purpose of this meeting is to help each other to remain clean and sober. If you are under the influence of drugs or alcohol now, we ask that you not speak at this meeting. Members are available before and after the meeting to talk with you and answer questions. Everything we share in these meetings is to be kept in absolute confidence. Please respect the needs of those who wish to speak by limiting your sharing time, if that appears to be necessary. There will be (45/60) minutes of sharing, followed by (10/15) minutes of open discussion (better known as cross talk).

From Glendale, California:

Welcome to SOS. My name is _____. I have been asked to lead tonight's meeting. Secular Organizations for Sobriety (or Save Our Selves) is dedicated to providing a path to sobriety, an alternative to those paths depending upon supernatural or religious beliefs. We respect diversity, welcome healthy skepticism, and encourage rational thinking as well as the expression of feelings. We each take responsibility for our individual sobriety on a daily basis.

This is a sobriety meeting. Our focus is on the priority of abstaining from alcohol and other mind-altering drugs. We respect the anonymity of each person in this room. This is a self-help, non-professional group. At this meeting, we share our experiences, understandings, thoughts, and feelings.

Announcements: Ask for announcements from the group. Announce new literature, meeting schedules, etc. Indicate if coffee or refreshments are available and if smoking is allowed. Ask for report on the treasury.

Anniversaries: We celebrate various lengths of sobriety in these meetings. Is there anyone here with less than thirty days of sobriety? Is there anyone here with thirty days of continuous sobriety? Sixty days? Three months? Six months? Nine months? Is there anyone celebrating a yearly anniversary this week? If you have an anniversary date coming up, please let me know after the meeting, and we will prepare a celebration for that date.

Reading: Tonight I have asked _____ to read the Suggested Guidelines for Sobriety. [Reads.]

Introductions: Again, I'm _____. Now, starting with the person on my left, let's introduce ourselves.

Opening: This meeting is now open. We ask that you try to keep your sharing to a reasonable length of time so that everyone can participate.

Closing: This group is self-supporting. If you can make some contribution, we will use it to help defray the cost of rent, refreshments, and other expenses. (Pass the basket.) Does anyone have any input for the central Clearinghouse monthly report? Sobriety is our priority and we each assume the responsibility for our lives and our sobriety. Thank you for coming and please come back. Let's close by giving ourselves a hand for being here to support and celebrate each other's sobriety.

From Rochester, N.Y.

Hello, it's time to begin. Welcome to SOS. My name is _____and I will lead tonight's meeting. Secular Organizations for Sobriety, or Save Our Selves, is dedicated to providing a path to sobriety and is an alternative to those that emphasize or depend upon supernatural or religious beliefs. We respect diversity, welcome healthy skepticism, and encourage rational thinking as well as expression of feelings. We each take responsibility for our individual sobriety on a daily basis. This is a sobriety meeting. Our focus is on the priority of abstaining from alcohol and other mind-altering drugs.

Announcements: Literature availability, refreshments, no smoking, purpose of contributions

Anniversaries: Does anyone have a sobriety anniversary they wish to have us celebrate?

We consider religion or spirituality to be separate issues. We choose to use the following guidelines to achieve our goal of abstinence from our drug of choice.

Six Guidelines: (read by another attendee)

We will now go around the room and introduce ourselves. Please use your first name only. When you introduce yourself, you may wish to mention some recent crisis or event in your life, or you may simply "pass." Please be brief at this point. We will get back to you, if you wish, after we have heard from everyone. We feel that the observations from the group might be of value to you, but if you don't want comments, please tell us so.

Again, my name is_____ and the person on my left/right is?

Closing: We have a telephone list from which you may copy names and numbers and/or add your own. Ask to see the list after the meeting.

We respect the anonymity of everyone at this meeting. What you hear and who you see should remain here. You may tell others that you attend SOS. It is not acceptable for you to say that I do. In this group there is hope for recovery from the frustration, the despair, and the isolation most of us have known as a result of our addiction. Sobriety is our priority, and we each assume the responsibility for our lives and our sobriety. Thank you for coming. Please come back.

Let's close by standing and joining hands to give each other support and celebrate our sobriety.

Sample Meeting Topics

(Collected from Tuesday and Thursday
Oakland Meetings, 1996-97)

Accepting things I can't change

Addictive Thinking

Anger

Awareness of my own self and feelings

Blame

Booze, violence and sex

Change

Changes we can make in our behavior

Changing my environment

Control

Death

Denial

Dependence

Falling back into old patterns

Fear

Feelings

Getting Real

Grieving

Guilt

Happiness

Honesty

How to survive the Christmas holiday

Hungry, angry, lonely and tired

Jim Christopher's Triumph workshop

Joy

Little lies

Meetings as a life line

My program for the Sobriety Priority

My story that brought me here

Pain

Parenting

Progress in Recovery

Recovery

Relapse

Relationships

Responsibility

Returning to work

Scary things

Secularism

Serendipity

Shame

Sobriety

Stress

Taking responsibility

Thoughts and words

Triggers and cravings

Trust

Values

What brought me to recovery

What brought me to SOS

What I am thankful for

What kind of user am I?

What SOS means to me

Sample Meeting Signup Sheet

SOS of (City), Monday Night Meeting
(Location) Optional Signup Sheet Date _____

Name	Phone	Name	Phone
_____ _____	_____ _____
_____ _____	_____ _____
_____ _____	_____ _____
_____ _____	_____ _____
_____ _____	_____ _____
_____ _____	_____ _____
_____ _____	_____ _____
_____ _____	_____ _____
_____ _____	_____ _____

Mtg Secy: _____   Treas:_____

Chair: _____ Chair Next Week: _____

Topic:_____

$ Donated: _____

Books Borrowed: Borrower:

_____ _____

_____ _____

Sample New Meeting Flyer

Had Enough?

There is a new self-help support group for recovering alcoholics in the [City] area!

S.O.S.
Secular Organizations for Sobriety/ Save Our Selves

If you seek recovery from a problem with alcohol or drugs, but are uncomfortable with the spiritual content of widely available 12-step programs, the alternative is Secular Organizations for Sobriety. SOS takes a rational, secular approach to recovery – without religion – based on individual responsibility and the Sobriety Priority.

Every [Day of Week] [Time], [Room], [Building] [Street Address, City, Zip]
[Directions if necessary]

For more information about the new meeting, contact [local contact person] at [local telephone number].

For more information about SOS, contact the SOS International Clearinghouse, 5521 Grosvenor Boulevard, Los Angeles, CA 90066, telephone (310) 821-8430.

Visit SOS on the Internet:
http://www.unhooked.com

Sample Press Release

FOR IMMEDIATE RELEASE
Sobriety Group To Add New Local Chapter

Secular Organizations for Sobriety, a support organization for people recovering from alcohol and drug abuse, has added a new local group. Meetings will be held every [day of week] night, beginning March 20th, [year] at [time] P.M. in [room] of [building], on [street address], in the [neighborhood] area of [town].

SOS, also known as "Save Our Selves," was founded by Jim Christopher in 1986 in North Hollywood, California. It is a friendly alternative to such organizations as Alcoholics Anonymous, which many people feel have a religious/spiritual basis to their recovery program. S.O.S. takes a secular approach, emphasizing that each individual must draw upon his or her own resources to deal with the problems of addiction---hence the name "Save Our Selves." S.O.S. chapters are meeting throughout the United States and abroad.

SOS also meets locally every [weekday] night at [time] at [other details].

For further information about the new meeting, contact [name of local contact person] at [local telephone number]. For further information about SOS, contact the SOS International Clearinghouse in Los Angeles at (310) 821-8430. Also visit SOS on the Internet at www.unhooked.com.

-30-

Specimen Letter to Professionals

SOS/Secular Organizations for Sobriety/Save Our Selves
[City] Area Chapter
[P.O. Box] [City, Zip]

[Name of Professional]
[Agency]
[Street]
[City, Zip]

Dear Sir or Ms:

This letter is to inform you of the availability of an alcohol/addiction recovery support group for your consideration as an alternative referral entity for appropriate chemical dependency patients. SOS (Secular Organizations for Sobriety) was founded in 1986, and has become an international movement. Local groups have regular sobriety meetings where anyone desiring abstinence from alcohol or addictive drugs is welcome. Please refer to the attached meeting schedule.

SOS meetings differ from traditional religious-based, 12-step meetings (i.e., AA, NA, etc.) in that religion is considered a separate issue. Individuals are encouraged to take responsibility (with help from others) for their own recovery just as they would for diabetes or other illness.

While some individuals do best with a religious or spiritual approach, there are many who, for various reasons, prefer to leave religion out of it or deal with their religious beliefs separately. For your reference, the Spring 1996 issue of the *Journal of Drug and Alcohol Abuse* carries an article, "Characteristics of Participants in Secular Organization for Sobriety (SOS)". Also, you may want to look over "Matching Alcoholism Treatments to Client Heterogeneity: Project MATCH Posttreatment Drinking Outcomes" in the January, 1997 issue of *Journal of Studies on Alcohol*, wherein secular approaches to treatment are shown to be equally valid as 12-Step based approaches.

We feel we have had good results. We would like to encourage you to consider offering SOS along with other options to your patients seeking long-term recovery. For further information on the local groups, please telephone the undersigned at [local phone number]. Or you may contact the SOS International Clearinghouse at (310) 821-8430. Or you may visit SOS on the Internet at www.unhooked.com.

Thank you for your professional attention to this matter,

Sincerely yours,

[Local Contact Person]

Enclosure: Meeting Schedule

General Principles of SOS

All those who sincerely seek sobriety are welcome as members in any SOS group.

SOS is not a spin-off of any religious group. There is no hidden agenda, as SOS is concerned with sobriety, not religiosity.

SOS seeks only to promote sobriety amongst those who suffer from alcoholism or other drug addictions. As a group, SOS has no opinion on outside matters and does not wish to become entangled in outside controversy.

Although sobriety is an individual responsibility, life does not have to be faced alone. The support of other alcoholics and addicts is a vital adjunct to recovery. In SOS, members share experiences, insights, information, strength, and encouragement in friendly, honest, anonymous, and supportive group meetings.

To avoid unnecessary entanglements, each SOS group is self-supporting through contributions from its members, and refuses outside support.

Sobriety is the number one priority in an alcoholic's or addict's life. As such, they must abstain from all drugs or alcohol.

Honest, clear, and direct communication of feelings, thoughts, and knowledge aids in recovery and in choosing non-destructive, non-delusional, and rational approaches to living sober and rewarding lives.

As knowledge of drinking or addiction might cause a person harm or embarrassment in the outside world, SOS guards the anonymity of its membership and the contents of its discussions from those not within the group.

SOS encourages the scientific study of alcoholism and addiction in all their aspects. SOS does not limit its outlook to one area of knowledge or theory of alcoholism or other addiction.

SOS On the Internet

The SOS Email List: A Sober Place In Cyberspace

Secular sobriety support delivered to your computer daily. The SOS freethought forum on the Internet. Email to **tshelley@gte.net** to join.

The SOS Home Page in San Francisco
www.unhooked.com

Meeting List, local and national – News of SOS – Onramp to Email List – Email Keepers – Sobriety Education Project Live Reading List – Sobriety Toolbox – Links – Library – Humor – Other Features. Updated Weekly.

The SOS Convenor's Home Page
http://home1.gte.net/markp/index.htm

For SOS meeting secretaries, treasurers, and others in service positions.

SOS on AOL

Keyword A&R | Message Center | Support Groups | Browse Folders | SOS

SOS in the UK
www.lewisham.gov.uk/volorgs/sos/

The SOS organization in England.

The SOS International Newsletter

James Christopher, Editor. Published four times a year.

From recent issues:

SOS Europe: Meetings Spread Throughout the United Kingdom, Paris, and Brussels — Retreat Brings Organizational Changes — More Power to Your Neo-Cortex (Spring, 1997).

SOS Down Under: Australian Outreach Project — A Funny Thing Happened to Me On the Way to the Drug Store (Winter 1996-97).

SOS Prisoner Outreach: Founder Visits Texas System — Reach Out and Touch Someone — Working With Others — My SOS One-Two-Three (Fall 1996).

Regular features: *Modem Memoranda* by Tom Shelley, *Wind Beneath My Wings* by Valerie White, SOS Newsbriefs, Mailbox, Marketplace.

Subscription Coupon

__ 1 year $18.00 ___2 years $32.00 __ 3 years, $45. __ . Donation_____

___Check or money order enclosed. __ Charge my __ MasterCard __ Visa

Card # _____ Expires_____

Name:

_____Signature_____

Address:_____

Daytime phone: (___) _____

City: _____

State _____ Zip _____

Mail to SOS Newsletter, Box 5, Buffalo, NY 14215-0005

Other Literature of SOS

Brochures

Recovery for Families and Friends -- A new brochure offering guidelines for families and friends of alcoholics and addicts.

Save Our Selves -- The basic overview brochure of the SOS movement. Includes the principles and history of SOS.

Your First Thirty Days -- Information and advice for the newly sober alcoholic or addict, includes list of suggested books to read.

The Sobriety Priority -- Excerpted from Christopher's book, *How To Stay Sober*, this brochure explains the Sobriety Priority of the SOS philosophy.

All available from the Clearinghouse *at $0.10 each in quantities of 50 or more.*

SOS Journal of Recovery

A diary and Daily-Do exercise booklet for each day in your first year of sobriety. With brief introductory text and thoughts for each week. $6.95 each, $4.95 in bulk, including postage & handling.

Audiotapes

Avoiding the Relapse Mode by Jim Christopher. Discusses Jim's own relapse prevention techniques and case histories of others' achievement of a comfortable sobriety. 30 minutes, $7.95 incl. postage & handling.

(Continued on page 96)

(Continued from page 95)

Empowerment Sobriety by Jim Christopher. Candid look at the Sobriety Priority method as exemplified by Jim and other case histories. 30 mins, $7.95 incl. postage & handling.

Videotapes

SOS Group Leader's Guide -- The Video. Videotape based on 1990 Group Leader's Guidebook for new convenors. How to launch a group, where to meet, how to promote, how to poise the group for growth. Complete suggested format and more, all demonstrated on camera by experienced SOS convenors, role-playing a meeting for you. 45 mins, $39.95 plus $2.00 postage & handling.

The Sobriety Priority. This professionally produced video is ideal for presentation of SOS to the general public or on cable TV. 1990. 14 mins., $24.95 & $2.00 postage & handling.

Available through the SOS International Clearinghouse, 5521 Grosvenor Boulevard, Los Angeles, CA 90066; Tel (310) 821-8430, Fax (310) 821-2610.

Books by James Christopher

How to Stay Sober: Recovery Without Religion. The book that started an international grass roots movement. SOS founder James Christopher describes his own "recovery without religion," focuses on the practical aspects of his triumph over alcoholism, and includes guidelines for the formation of secular support groups. 191 pages, $15.95/18.95. Prometheus Books, N.Y. 1988. ISBN 0-87975-457-5.

Unhooked: Staying Sober and Drug Free. James Christopher recounts the evolution of SOS and details cases of recovery through the program. He invites the reader to sit in on a fictionalized SOS meeting, and offers further strategies for achieving and maintaining sobriety and self-respect. 184 pages, $15.95/16.95. Prometheus Books, N.Y. 1989. ISBN 0-87975-564-4.

SOS Sobriety: The Proven Alternative to 12-Step Programs. James Christopher lays bare the limitations of Alcoholics Anonymous while describing the proven methods of alcohol and drug abstention used by Secular Organizations for Sobriety. After answering basic questions about SOS, the book documents the success of the "sobriety priority" approach through two scientific studies. 240 pages, $15.95/16.95. Prometheus Books, N.Y. 1992. ISBN 0-87975-726-4.

First price quoted is for purchases via the SOS International Clearinghouse, 5521 Grosvenor Boulevard, Los Angeles, CA 90066; Tel (310) 821-8430, Fax (310) 821-2610. Second price is via bookstores or the publisher.

Index

Notes

Order Blank

Please send **Sobriety Handbook: The SOS Way** to:

Name: _____

Street: _____

City: _____ State:___ ZIP: _____

Number of copies: _____

Price: $10 per copy
Add $2 shipping for first copy, $4 for
packages of 2-5 via first class mail.
California residents add 8.25 % sales tax.

Call or Write for
SOS Meeting Discounts

Order directly from

LifeRing Press

* **By phone: 510-763-0779, 24 hours.**
* **By fax: 510-763-1513, 24 hours.**
* **By mail:**
    LifeRing Press
    1440 Broadway Suite 1000B
    Oakland CA 94612-2029
* **By email: lifering@unhooked.com**
* **On the Web:**
    www.unhooked.com/lifering/